Penguin Critical Studies
Joint Advisory Editors:
Stephen Coote and Bryan Loughrey

Chaucer

The Nun's Priest's Tale

Stephen Coote

Penguin Books

PENGUIN BOOKS

Published by the Penguin Group
27 Wrights Lane, London W8 5TZ, England
Viking Penguin Inc., 40 West 23rd Street, New York, New York 10010, USA
Penguin Books Australia Ltd, Ringwood, Victoria, Australia
Penguin Books Canada Ltd, 2801 John Street, Markham, Ontario, Canada L3R 1B4
Penguin Books (NZ) Ltd, 182–190 Wairau Road, Auckland 10, New Zealand

Penguin Books Ltd, Registered Offices: Harmondsworth, Middlesex, England

First published in Penguin Masterstudies 1985
Reprinted in Penguin Critical Studies 1989
10 9 8 7 6 5 4 3 2 1

Made and printed in Great Britain by
Richard Clay Ltd, Bungay, Suffolk
Filmset in Monophoto Times

Contents

Introduction

The Nun's Priest's Tale is a beast fable. In this respect it is like *Animal Farm* or *Tom and Jerry*. Indeed, it has strong similarities to both. *Animal Farm* is serious. It tells how a group of agricultural creatures, feeling themselves exploited, revolt under the leadership of the pigs, expel the humans and set up a communist state. We recognize the story as an allegory at once. Napoleon – the head pig – represents Stalin, Snowball represents Trotsky, while the carthorse Boxer stands for the ordinary labouring man. Of course, the animals' revolt develops into a tyranny. Its leaders become more and more like the once despised humans, until, in the end – and in a phrase that shows how readily we use animals to encapsulate human attributes – Napoleon becomes no more than a 'capitalist pig'. *Tom and Jerry*, on the other hand, is raucous. The cartoon pictures a menacing yet lovable cat who is taunted by Jerry the mouse. The action is vigorously knockabout, and the mouse – rather like the hero of Chaucer's story – escapes from danger by an enviable combination of cool and good luck.

The Nun's Priest's Tale, playing on the ancient need to see human life in animal terms, combines these elements of seriousness and farce. In it we are introduced to Chauntecleer, scholar and cock of the walk, to Pertelote his wife, to the Widow who owns them and to Russel the fox who tries to make off with the comic hero. That all these figures suggest influential medieval ideas is soon obvious. Defining what those ideas are will be a main purpose of this Introduction. But it is important to remember that *The Nun's Priest's Tale* remains both very funny and very delightful. By a paradox that will become clearer as we progress, it is precisely because it is so amusing that the Tale is also serious. However, before we can examine the work in detail, we need to know something about its author and the world in which he lived.

1. An Approach to Chaucer

Chaucer and the culture of the fourteenth-century court

'The past', wrote the novelist L. P. Hartley, 'is a foreign country: they do things differently there.' It is these differences we should be aware of if our criticism of Chaucer's work is to avoid being anachronistic. We need to know something about medieval Europe and the ways in which Chaucer's story relates to its life and thought. Only then can we see both the Tale and its author making a timeless comment on human folly.

Our readiest entry to the medieval world is through Chaucer's life. The date of his birth is unknown but is generally fixed at around 1340. His parents were prosperous wine merchants, and it seems possible that Chaucer received his first education at a London grammar school. However that may be, by 1357 he had become attached to the household of the Countess of Ulster. The move was of the greatest importance to his poetry, for it meant that to his experience of the middle-class world of business affairs – a world with which he was never to lose contact – Chaucer could add a knowledge of the life of the aristocracy. We need to pay some attention to this, for the court was a centre both of poetry and of European culture, while the life of the princely is humorously analysed in the life of Chauntecleer – the prince of the Widow's back yard.

The daily existence of the medieval aristocracy was formal, lavish and highly colourful. As a page or squire in the household of a great family – and later at the court of Edward III himself – Chaucer's duties included waiting on his masters in the livery they had provided, serving at table, kneeling with water bowls so that fingers could be washed after a meal, and valeting clothes. When promoted to service with the king, he and his fellows were required 'to make beddis, to beare or hold torches, to sett boardis [tables], to apparell all Chambers, and other such Services as the Chamberlaine, or Ushers of Chambre commaunde or assigne; to attend the Chambre; to watche the King by course; to goe in messages'. In this way, by observing the court and its pageantry, Chaucer came to know intimately the ceremony and etiquette that surrounded the existence of the great. He had entered a world of highly formalized life and conspicuous public display. The lavishness and colour of this should be borne in mind when we think of Chauntecleer 'thus royal, as a prince is in his halle'. Again, while Pertelote is only a farmyard chicken, when we remember that she is also Chauntecleer's queen, then we can gauge something of Chaucer's comic effect when we compare her self-importance to Edward III's ordering a tunic for his wife that was worked with birds of gold, each of which was surrounded by a wide circle of pearls – some four hundred in all – besides the 38 oz of lesser pearls that were sewn on to the background. The comparison may make us smile at the dust-bathing Pertelote's farmyard pretensions, but it should also make us think that the royal world, thick with ceremony and brocade, was just as fallible as life in the Widow's hencoop.

The court was the centre of power, and authority was personified in the king. Under Edward III the English court had become famous throughout Europe. A chronicler described the royal face shining like a god's and added that to see him, or even to dream of him, was to conjure up joyous images. All of this was conventional. Frequently such images as came to the writer's mind were of a mythical past – of Arthur and the Round Table perhaps – for in the feudal society of the middle ages an elaborate ideal of aristocratic life dominated ethical and political thought. The social order, it was believed, had been determined by God, and the supremacy of princes had a divine justification. The highest tasks in the state belonged to such men by right. In turn, it was their duty to protect the church, succour the people and combat tyranny and violence. Born to such influence – regardless of how they exercised it – the nobility decorated their lives with a vision of their own splendour and imitated an ideal past. The heroes of history and literature inspired them to chivalry, kindled a longing for praise, and awoke the desire for fame. Such dreams even had a part to play in real life. Richard II, together with his uncles, the Dukes of Lancaster, York and Gloucester, challenged the King of France and his uncles to settle their differences by personal combat. Later, Henry V was similarly to challenge the Dauphin before the Battle of Agincourt. In 1425, the Duke of Burgundy dared the Duke of Gloucester to a duel so that 'by my own body, this quarrel may be settled, without proceeding by means of wars, which would entail many noblemen and others, both of your army and mine, ending their days pitifully'. To act by such notions as these was to see politics and history as matters of family status and personal pride. And it is through just these that Russel the fox appeals to the princely Chauntecleer. He reminds him of his father's prowess in crowing and panders to his inborn vanity. Both temptations reflect the shortcomings of the aristocracy in a feudal society. As the Nun's Priest himself comments:

> Allas! ye lordes, many a fals flatour
> Is in your courtes, and many a losengeour,
> That plesen yow wel more, by my feith,
> Than he that soothfastnesse unto yow seith.
> Redeth Ecclesiaste of flaterye;
> Beth war, ye lordes, of hir trecherye.

Pride, proverbially, must fall. The lives of medieval princes were a constant reminder of this. For some years the court of Edward III detained King John of France and his peers while they waited for their ransoms to be raised. The history of Burgundy is similarly full of violent reversals in the lives of its rulers, while, nearer home, Richard II, the irresponsible grandson of Edward III, was to be not only deposed but secretly murdered. It is thus not surprising that one of the dominant images of medieval art and thought is that of Fortune's wheel constantly turning, raising up some and casting others down. This concept of Fortune, though handled in a comic way, is central to *The Nun's Priest's Tale*. Chauntecleer, full of pride, struts to his fall. Russel the fox, having got his victim apparently in his grasp, immediately loses him. As the Nun's Priest again comments:

> Lo, how fortune turneth sodeinly
> The hope and pryde eek of hir enemy.

In *The Nun's Priest's Tale* Fortune's wheel turns and then turns again. All things – even cocks and foxes – are subject to its power. And, as we shall see, this notion of Fortune affects many of the poem's other themes. For example, not only is it central to the analysis given of Chauntecleer's pride, but his long discourse on the nature of dreams is designed to show that such things are a valid warning of future catastrophe. His wife dismisses these ideas as ridiculous. The old and patient Widow is roused to desperate action by the fox's sudden attack on her domestic economy. Even the style of the poem is affected by the theme of Fortune. Many of the passages in which Fortune is invoked serve to parody a long tradition of pomposity in such verse. Indeed, *The Nun's Priest's Tale* itself is a criticism of the work which precedes it; the Monk's lengthy and tedious list of those who learned to their cost how

> fortune alwey wol assaille
> With unwar strook the regnes that ben proude

unwar: unforeseen *regnes*: kings

Such histories were facts of common observation in the courts of medieval Europe.

Medieval courtly life was thus often violent, cruel and extreme. Robes and furred gowns offered little protection from political truths. Rather, they enhanced the ambitions of those who ruled. 'Princes are men,' wrote the chronicler Chastellain, 'and their affairs are high and perilous, their natures are subject to many passions ... their hearts are veritable dwelling-places of these, because of their pride in reigning.' He could almost have been describing Chauntecleer himself as he struts about his little realm, his natural colours as gaudy as heraldry and his bearing too lofty 'to sette his foot to grounde'. It is partly with such sentiments as these in mind – the proud but uncertain tenor of courtly life – that we should view

Chaucer's cockerel puffing himself up, beating his wings, and stretching out his princely neck to sing. As he prepares to display his foolish glory, so he exposes himself to the fox. To the medieval belief that such Pride as his was the chief of the Seven Deadly Sins we shall have frequently to return.

Chaucer the poet

(i) LANGUAGE, ORAL LITERATURE, SOME THEMES IN THE EARLIER POEMS

Despite such pomp and insecurity – or perhaps because of them – English court life was both intricate and highly civilized. Royal display demanded art, and money was lavished on magnificence. The King of France, living in the English court, might have been a hostage to fortune, but he did not spend his time in penal servitude. He was an honoured guest surrounded by his own retinue. One of his peers was accompanied by no less than sixteen servants. The noble prisoners were amazed at the lavishness of the feasts they attended and were beguiled by tournaments – which it is likely Chaucer attended – that were partly paid for by their own ransacked gold.

The presence of these Frenchmen in the English court serves to underline a matter of great significance. English artistic life – its poetry in particular – was dominated by French forms. There is a clear historical reason for this. The Norman Conquest had ensured that Norman French became the language of rulers and administrators. (It remained the written language of the law until the early eighteenth century.) French thus became the dominant medium of secular culture. The native speech of the conquered Saxons – which had developed its own remarkable literature – was quickly reduced to a merely spoken tongue, subject to all the impermanence and vulnerability of a language without a written record. The triumph of French vocabulary and French grammar meant that England was now part of a cultural world that had as its centres the Loire and the Seine. And, in adopting its grammatical forms, the country adopted its artistic ones too. Intellectual and literary life in England during the twelfth and thirteenth centuries was expressed mainly in French – as well as the Latin of the church – and the influence of these two tongues was to be considerable for many generations to come. However, the changing, very flexible native language began slowly to merge with French and Latin – gaining hugely in vocabulary, range and usefulness – until, in 1362, when Chaucer was in his early twenties, Parliament was opened in English for the first time. Chaucer's unique historical importance lies in the fact that, more than any other individual poet, he rose to the challenge of reinterpreting the inheritance of continental literature in the newly rich diversity of his native language. For this reason – if for no other – he is rightly regarded as 'the father of English literature'.

The court itself remained bilingual and maintained contacts with a wide variety of cultures from Paris to Prague. It is important to remember that Chaucer was not only familiar with French literature, but was also well read in the Latin classics, and, as he rose to be entrusted on diplomatic missions, came to know the poetry of Italy as well. Such a breadth of literary experience was part of his training. As a squire – and in addition to the somewhat menial duties already described – Chaucer was required to entertain his royal patrons with readings from French literature and, whenever necessary, with recitations from his own compositions. This last fact raises a number of important issues.

First of all it suggests the oral nature of medieval poetry. An exquisite contemporary manuscript illustration shows Chaucer standing at a lectern and reading aloud to the aristocratic audience which formed a large part but, as we shall see, far from the whole body of his admirers. The courtiers are listeners rather than readers, and this makes their experience of literature rather different to ours. We are used to reading as a solitary activity. We are used to long and intricate passages of prose given to us in printed form from the pens of authors whom – in all likelihood – we have never met. For Chaucer's audience however, litera-ture was often a communal activity depending more on the ear than the eye. Because someone listening to a recitation cannot turn back the pages to refer to what may have been forgotten and also because the ear needs a variety and range of sound if it is to remain alert, such verse as Chaucer's is both highly patterned and widely diverse. *The Nun's Priest's Tale* is a particularly good example of this.

The formal patterning of poetry – the proper term is rhetoric – was a highly prized and elaborate skill. It had the most complex rules and was a central part of what we now refer to as higher education. Of course, rhetoric had an important purpose. To all who had to communicate – priests, lawyers, propagandists, poets and others – it provided clear rules on how to capture an audience's attention and persuade them to a particular point of view. But rules can become rigid and ridiculous. They develop mannerisms. Chaucer was perfectly well aware of this and, in *The Nun's Priest's Tale*, we shall see that he satirizes the more absurd aspects of medieval rhetorical technique. This is again a crucial part of his comic effect.

One of the reasons why Chaucer knew that rhetoric for its own sake is ineffective is that he relished the variety of spoken language. Listen to the scathing exchanges in the 'Prologue' to *The Nun's Priest's Tale* or the earthy sarcasm of Pertelote:

> 'Avoy!' quod she, 'fy on yow, hertelees!
> Allas!' quod she, 'for, by that god above,
> Now han ye lost myn herte and al my love;
> I can nat love a coward, by my feith.'

This is henpecking indeed. Later, when we examine more of the range of Chaucer's language in the Tale, we shall see that it includes the tenderly descriptive, the sententious and epigrammatic, a skill with ironic aside, and, where necessary, a considerable abstract subtlety. But the language always relates to the ear. It is always designed for a listening audience, often a courtly, sophisticated and pleasure-loving one such as that in the manuscript illustration.

Before the age of printing, the oral culture we have been describing was based on the manuscript, and manuscripts were expensive and often beautiful. It took a flock of three or four hundred sheep to provide parchment for a lengthy volume – a complete *Canterbury Tales*, perhaps – and the best books were themselves great works of art, their illustrations colourful with jewel-like intensity and remarkably sophisticated in the handling of line, drapery and pictorial effect. The great 'carpet pages' of *Queen Mary's Psalter* are splendid things, profuse in ornament and grotesques, while, in the borders of such works as the *Luttrell Psalter* (*c.* 1340), we see an attractive love of contemporary detail: lords and ladies, peasants and animals. The hieratic solemnity with which the middle ages graced the serious issues of life and salvation was, at its best, offset by a vivid sense of observation and sheer humorous delight. We should bear this constantly in mind when we discuss *The Nun's Priest's Tale*.

The Tale itself, of course, is part of a far larger collection, but it may be useful if we first place *The Canterbury Tales* themselves in the context of Chaucer's previous work. In so doing, we shall see that *The Nun's Priest's Tale* deals with some of Chaucer's abiding artistic concerns.

It is significant of the state of literary life in fourteenth-century England that what was probably Chaucer's first work was a partial translation of a poem by two Frenchmen. The *Roman de la Rose* by Guillaume de Lorris and the more cynical Jean de Meung is one of the seminal works of European culture. It is a long piece – over 20,000 lines – whose historical importance perhaps outweighs what can now be readily appreciated of its literary merits. Like *The Nun's Priest's Tale*, it too is an allegory – an allegory about love. The poem takes the form of a dream vision in which a young man – an aristocrat, of course – finds himself in a garden and falls in love with a rose – in other words a beautiful young girl. Numerous figures portraying the various stages in courtship approach him, and the whole work is, in its own terms, a subtle essay in medieval emotional analysis. What we need to be concerned with here are its tone of high sophistication for the most part and its analysis of aristocratic passion.

The *Roman de la Rose* provided the vocabulary for a central preoccupation of medieval literature: the conventional ardours of idealized emotion that we now term 'courtly love'. This vocabulary, developing the work of the troubadour poets of twelfth-century Provence, pictured the beloved lady as remote, disdainful and the seat of all virtue. She became a near improbable idealization to be won by great labour and immense patience. In her service the lover perfected himself. His lady became the centre and inspiration of all his bravery and social finesse. Such a pattern of behaviour is the subject of much of Chaucer's work. What we may call his first original poem – *The Book of the Duchess* – is greatly concerned with formal praise and the long pursuit of an ideal lady. Amongst *The Canterbury Tales* themselves, the tales of the Knight and the Franklin are centred on such idealism, but they discuss it – somewhat unusually for the time – in terms of marriage, the sacrament that gave lovers a recognized place in adult society and the only legitimate status within the church's teaching on sex.

In what is perhaps the greatest of Chaucer's complete works – *Troilus and Criseyde* – the pursuit of courtly love is again described with great elaboration and through the most penetratingly observed characterization. *Troilus and Criseyde* is a tragedy, the plot of which Chaucer discovered in the work of the Italian poet Boccaccio. It is set in an entirely un-Homeric version of the Trojan war, a favourite imaginative locale of medieval writers. The poem tells how the love of Troilus for Criseyde fell fro wo to wele, and after out of Ioye', and, in recounting his unhappy adventures, the idea of Fortune's revolving wheel is again crucial. While the characters in the poem are indeed vividly portrayed – Troilus, young, ardent and at first naïve; Criseyde, delightfully complex and feminine; her uncle Pandarus, lively, gossiping and worldly wise – one of the poem's principal concerns is to present these highly literary creations in a philosophical setting that explores the relationships between human desire, Fortune and free will. In other words, the poet asks: does man control his own destiny or is he a mere puppet of fate. To what does desire lead and may man know the future? These are crucial themes in many of Chaucer's mature works · not least *The Nun's Priest's Tale* – and, as we shall see, they were major preoccupations of many thinking men of his day as well.

Chaucer's immediate source for his discussion of Fortune was a Latin work from the very end of the classical period: *The Consolation of Philosophy* by Boethius. In this book – which Chaucer himself translated – the imprisoned Boethius, deprived of the honours heaped on him by his fickle emperor, discusses with the allegorical figure of Philosophy ideas of good and evil, the nature of happiness, Fortune and free will. The work shows a profound knowledge of the instability of earthly existence and a longed-for sense of benevolent order that man can attain to once he has passed beyond worldly attachments. And it is these latter – Troilus's emotions as he first falls in love with Criseyde, discovers earthly happiness and then has it snatched from him when Criseyde is sent back to her father and deserts her lover for another man – around which Chaucer's tragedy is constructed. Near the close of the work, the heart-broken Troilus meditates on the themes that Boethius had discussed, but in his wretchedness cannot find a clear way to understanding them. All he knows is that Fortune rules earthly attachments and is fickle and cruel to those who place their faith in earthly things.

It is obvious that *The Nun's Priest's Tale* is concerned with similar themes of Fortune and love – Chauntecleer is a victim both of destiny and his own pride and concupiscence – but it is also clear that the Tale deals with these ideas in a wholly different way. First, *The Nun's Priest's Tale* concerns itself with married love. Chauntecleer and Pertelote are, we are asked to believe, man and wife. This is a crucial distinction and it allowed Chaucer to present the relation between his hero and heroine in the most shrewd and comic manner. Thus, while in some of Chauntecleer's speeches to his wife we hear a little of the courtesy of formalized emotion that courtly love required – and which was conventionally associated with princes and others of high birth – Pertelote's down-to-earth language and her husband's need for sexual release provide a rich contrast to this and so suggest a variety of responses within marriage. This variety is both engaging and realistic. It is through its comedy that we come to perceive Chauntecleer and Pertelote very much as a married couple, while, as we shall see later, the fact that they are indeed married allowed Chaucer to pursue ideas about the relation of man to wife and the place of sexual desire in wedlock in considerable and fascinating detail. Obviously, these are complex and important matters that we can only discuss fully when we have more information at our disposal, and it will be more helpful here if we look at another and obvious difference between *Troilus and Criseyde* and *The Nun's Priest's Tale*: the fact that the latter work is a comedy which concerns animals.

This form of literature – we have seen that its proper name is the 'beast fable' – was again one of Chaucer's abiding artistic interests. Two of his early poems exploit aspects of it. *The House of Fame* – the strange and unfinished work Chaucer started after *The Book of the Duchess* – contains the first of Chaucer's true comic figures: a delightfully garrulous eagle, a know-all who takes the poet on a long interplanetary flight and provides a humorous description of Chaucer's supposedly shy and bookish ways. The poem with which Chaucer followed this – *The Parliament of Fowls* – declares its ornithological interest in its title. It too helps us to define something of the world of *The Nun's Priest's Tale*, for, while its central concern is an elaborate debate about which of three eagles deserves to win the hand of the royal bird perched on the wrist of Dame Nature, the common birds in the poem grow increasingly impatient during the lengthy speeches and demand to be paired off. As far as they are concerned, the refinements of courtly love are all very well, but their main interest – like Chauntecleer's – is a powerful desire to procreate. This is perfectly natural, but, as we have mentioned, the place of sexual love within marriage and the relation between love of wife and love of God are also issues that deeply concern the Nun's Priest.

Finally, we should note that Chaucer's four earliest works – the translation of the *Roman de la Rose*, *The Book of the Duchess*, *The House of Fame* and *The Parliament of Fowls* are all dream visions. In each of these poems the Narrator, in a convention widely used in medieval literature, falls asleep and then tells us what he has seen. In *The Nun's Priest's Tale*, a long discussion on the nature of dreams lies close to the comic and thematic core of the work.

It is possible, then, to see *The Nun's Priest's Tale* drawing on a wide range of Chaucer's artistic preoccupations. The work is an allegory and a beast fable – forms which he had clearly enjoyed using in his early period as a poet – while, at the heart of the poem, lie some of the central themes of Chaucer's mature work, in particular married love, dreams, and man's relation to Fortune and free will. In addition, the remarkable skill Chaucer shows in orchestrating a wide variety of different voices suggests the technical achievements which, at the culmination of his career, he could bring to the work by which he is mostly widely and justly known: *The Canterbury Tales*.

(ii) THE CANTERBURY TALES

Reviewing the scope of *The Canterbury Tales*, the great seventeenth-century poet John Dryden declared that they contain 'God's plenty'. Let us see what he meant by this.

The Canterbury Tales, incomplete though it is, consists of tales and fragments told by the thirty-two pilgrims who have assembled at the

Tabard Inn in London before going on their journey to the shrine of St Thomas à Becket at Canterbury. They are joined by the Canon's Yeoman later in the journey. The purpose of pilgrimage we shall discuss in a moment, but the pilgrims themselves, who are described in *The General Prologue*, are one of the most convincing and lively groups of people gathered together in all literature. They come from a broad range of classes and backgrounds, and, though they have widely different attitudes to life, they have all assembled for a simple – and ostensibly religious – purpose.

In the opening paragraph of *The General Prologue*, Chaucer carefully prepares us for his portraits of representative types of medieval society by creating a famous impression of spring as a time of revived potency and love – love both religious and secular. Winter is over and the heart is stirring once more. People's minds turn to pilgrimage, to giving thanks or requesting the help of divine power. The depth and rectitude of Chaucer's pilgrims' faith varies widely, and his skill in portraying such a heterogeneous collection of people is an important aspect of his under-standing of the variety of human life. As we might expect, this diversity is reflected in his technique. Some of the characters – the Knight, the Ploughman and his brother the Parson, for example – are ideal types described in the conventional feudal terms of those who fight, those who labour and those who pray. They are all men of deep and attractive integrity, perfectly adjusted to their faith and the world in which they live. Chaucer also shows qualified admiration for some of the professional middle-class characters – the Franklin and the Sergeant-of-the-Law, for example – but among the most immediately attractive figures are the rogues: lapsed clerics such as the Monk and the Friar, or, even more, the Summoner and the Pardoner, the men who brought people before the law courts run by the church or who sold pardons respectively. Only two lengthy portraits of women are included in *The General Prologue*. First, the Wife of Bath, gaudy, amorous and socially aware; and secondly the large-boned, refined Prioress with her harmless little worldly vanities and entourage of a nun and three anonymous priests. It is one of these latter who tells the tale we are to discuss.

Pilgrims and pilgrimages

All of this cross-section of medieval society, at once individual and representative, the high-born and the lowly, the young and the middle-aged, the innocent and the villainous, the devout and the worldly, the sincere and the hypocritical, are within the fold of the Catholic church and are united by the ideals – or spurred by the hope of gain and adventure – which pilgrimage offered.

The concept of pilgrimage itself makes clear what is implicit both in the make-up of Chaucer's party and in many of the tales the pilgrims tell: the pervasive presence of the Catholic church in medieval England – its sacraments, language and wide variety of officials – and, more subtly perhaps, the all-embracing religious interpretation of human experience that the period enjoyed. The latter is particularly important, for, without giving due recognition to the fact that the people of the middle ages developed a marked tendency to relate worldly events to biblical and supernatural truths – quartering an apple, for example, could serve as a memento of the Trinity, the last part representing the Virgin's love of Jesus – then we shall fail to appreciate the particular use of such ways of thought that Chaucer introduces into *The Nun's Priest's Tale.* As we get a firmer purchase on the story, so the variety and subtle fascination of these ideas will become apparent, but we should notice here that even pilgrimage itself could become an image of a spiritual quest, an allegory of man's life, and there is something in the argument that holds that Chaucer shows the journey of man from London, the worldly Jerusalem, to Canterbury and its cathedral, the heavenly Jerusalem. If this idea does not take into account the fact that the pilgrims originally promised to return to the Tabard and wine and dine the teller of the best tale, the idea of a pilgrimage to Canterbury does, nonetheless, represent what was a widely practised activity in medieval England. Indeed, the shrine of St Thomas à Becket was the most popular in the whole country.

A number of things accounted for this. Thomas à Becket was murdered by four knights on the order of Henry II on 29 December 1170. The reason was political expedience. Becket had grown too powerful in his newly found role as a great churchman and threatened the power of his king with the international authority of the church. There were those – even after Becket's death – who regarded him as a traitor to his royal master, while others declared, naturally enough perhaps, that he was a martyr in the cause of the church's liberty. By the fourteenth century it was widely believed that the issue had been resolved by a supernatural umpire. As a contemporary declared: 'Christ has solved the problem by the manifold and great signs with which He has glorified him.' In other words, Becket's relics were declared to work miracles. Very soon, the cathedral at Canterbury had assembled the largest collection of miracle stories connected with a single shrine anywhere in the Europe of the middle ages. In addition, the country itself had acquired a hugely popular national saint.

The reason for St Thomas's popularity is both a clear and a moving one. The collected 'Miracles of Thomas à Becket' tell of down-to-earth comforts, of help, cures and benefits received, and, on the further shores of likelihood, the restoration of mutilated members and the raising of the dead. These accounts are the short and simple annals of those without an effective medical science and behind them lies the gratitude of the all-but-helpless for divine mercy. As Chaucer himself suggests, such gratitude is the reason for pilgrimage:

> ... from every shires ende
> Of Engelond, to Caunterbury they wende,
> The holy blisful martir for to seke,
> That hem hath holpen, whan that they were seke.

All of this was perfectly sincere, but we should not come away with the impression that Chaucer's imagined pilgrimage – or pilgrimages in general – were overwhelmingly solemn affairs. A deeply serious purpose underlay them, but, as we have seen, Chaucer's view of the relationship between the church and the characters he created was a subtle one. The pilgrims are all part of divine benevolence but many of them abuse their allotted places in it through personal weakness and professional deceit. And the abuse of pilgrimage itself was also well recognized and widely attacked. Pilgrimages were too often seen as occasions for illicit adventure. A character such as the Wife of Bath who goes on pilgrimages as much for company as anything else is in this a representative type as well as an imagined individual. Indeed, as the great religious writer Thomas à Kempis declared, those who go on pilgrimages rarely become saints.

The Canterbury Tales *as a collection of narratives*

Nonetheless, the idea of pilgrimage allowed Chaucer to bring together a wide and representative variety of characters and so create an image of medieval England more or less united by a religious purpose. It also allowed him to break free from the exclusive world of the aristocracy and exploit a range of poetic forms. The device was, further, a most convincing way of binding together a collection of narratives. By the apparently simple technique of gathering a heterogeneous collection of people in a public house and having them agree to tell stories under the rule of the publican Harry Bailey – stories that would divert or instruct them on a journey at once actual and symbolic – Chaucer could develop his art to its furthest extent.

The diversity of the tales the pilgrims tell mirrors their own variety and – in nearly all cases – the stories are appropriate to the nature and calling of those who tell them. If we divide the individual narratives into the 'genre' – or literary type – to which they belong, we find tragedy, romance, the fabliau or bawdy story and the saint's legend, while the Parson tells a sermon and *The Nun's Priest's Tale* suitably combines elements of this with the beast fable and other genres.

Though we should bear in mind that Chaucer died before his entire vast project was completed, if we ask ourselves how his contemporaries might have perceived both the whole plan and, just as significantly, those sections of it that remain, then we shall find that the possible answers throw much light on both the form of the tales themselves – *The Nun's Priest's Tale* in particular – and the expectations of the audience for whom the collection was composed.

It will be clear from what has already been said that *The Canterbury Tales* should not be considered too simply as the medieval equivalent of a modern collection of short stories. The concept of pilgrimage – its suggestion of a symbolic journey – at once argues for the work's particularly medieval nature, and, if we consider both the format of some of the manuscripts in which it survives and various aspects of the construction of *The Nun's Priest's Tale* itself, then we shall see that we are dealing here with a special kind of work, a specific type of literary compilation.

Many of the predominantly secular works that are preserved in large numbers – including such contemporary copies of *The Canterbury Tales* as the beautifully illuminated Ellsmere manuscript – suggest that such works were designed to appeal not just to an audience who required entertainment, but to one which sought instruction as well. Like the pilgrims themselves, Chaucer's contemporaries required both 'sentence', or teaching, as well as 'solas', or mirth. And it was part of the medieval poet's duty to pass on to his audience the wisdom of 'auctoritee' – the philosophy of the great figures of the past. In Chaucer's case, much of this material concerns his themes of Fortune, dreams, and desire, and, in the margins of the Ellsmere manuscript, there are headings to indicate who some of the authorities cited on these topics are. Thus, in certain respects, *The Canterbury Tales* was perceived by its audience – whether this was Chaucer's immediate intention or not – as a *compilatio*, a collection of wit and wisdom, philosophy and précis, such as preachers and, increasingly, educated members of the laity, were also familiar with. In this respect we can begin to see the lengthy asides on dreams and Fortune in *The Nun's Priest's Tale* not just as amusing passages in a delightful story – which they certainly are – nor just as comments on the action – which they certainly provide – but as part of a wider concern with rhetoric and information on topical problems which was desired by the more serious members of Chaucer's audience. It was such people as these, often members of a literate and highly intelligent lay middle class, who would have appreciated Chaucer's translation of Boethius and who were passionately concerned with many of the deeper issues of morality and salvation which Chaucer discusses in both *The Nun's Priest's Tale* and *The Canterbury Tales* as a whole.

We have now characterized Chaucer as a member of the articulate classes of the fourteenth century, a man with a searching and experimental interest in his native language and the literature of Europe. We have seen that he was writing in an oral culture for both the aristocracy and members of the educated administrative orders. We have seen that a number of themes central to *The Nun's Priest's Tale* – dreams, Fortune, free will, the place of sex within marriage, and such formal matters as the beast fable – were among Chaucer's abiding artistic concerns. We have also described something of the pervasive influence of courtly and ecclesiastical life on Chaucer's time and works. Finally, we have discussed pilgrimage and suggested its relation to *The Canterbury Tales*, viewing that marvellous work as both a special anthology of stories and a compilation of received wisdom. Having thus outlined something of the ambience within which Chaucer worked, we can now begin to discuss *The Nun's Priest's Tale* in more detail. We should start with the sources on which Chaucer drew for his narrative.

2. The Narrative Sources of *The Nun's Priest's Tale*

Chaucer's narrative is not an original one. It is his handling of received material – material both literary and popular – that is the supreme mark of his genius. This is a further indication of the difference between the past and ourselves. When we pick up a fictional narrative – a novel or a short story perhaps – we expect a more or less original plot. That plot may work within a convention – the detective story or science fiction, for example – but we are likely to be considerably disappointed if we are already familiar with the main thread of the events. That this was not the case with Chaucer's contemporaries raises a number of interesting points. It suggests, first of all, that a popular and much repeated tale was both enjoyed for its own sake and because it expressed some widely shared assumptions and conventional wisdom. In addition, the reworking of received material throws the balance of critical interest on to the means by which the narrative is handled: the differences, variations and additions which Chaucer made to what was already well known. It is in this area – the area of formal technique – that much of Chaucer's artistry lies, and, to appreciate it, we need to have some knowledge of previous versions of the story. As we have said, these earlier versions stem from both an intellectual literary tradition and from a popular and oral one, the presence of the latter being suggested by the frequent use of the motifs Chaucer employs in ecclesiastical wood and stone carving – and this during the period when the literary tradition of the story was more or less in abeyance. Such a use of motifs from popular culture is, as we shall see, a matter of importance in *The Nun's Priest's Tale*.

The literary tradition of *The Nun's Priest's Tale* stretches back to the Fables of Aesop, a sixth-century BC Phrygian slave whose works were for centuries used as school textbooks. Aesop tells a story of how a crow, sitting in a tree and eating a morsel of meat or cheese, was approached by a hungry fox who praised his plumage and declared that the crow would be the first among birds if only he could sing. The crow, much flattered at this, opened its beak to sing and consequently dropped his food, which the fox then greedily snapped up. Here is one motif from Chaucer's story: a bird beguiled by a fox's flattery of its voice.

Aesop's Fables were transmitted through Latin intermediaries and, in the ninth century, Alcuin of York wrote a Latin poem which suggests the second of the motifs in Chaucer's version: the bird's saving himself by a reciprocal flattery of the fox. In Alcuin's story, the bird has become a cockerel who has actually been caught by a wolf. Trapped in the wolf's maw, the cockerel cunningly declares that he does not mind being eaten so long as he can hear what he believes to be the wolf's wonderful voice. The wolf, much flattered, obligingly opens his mouth to show off, and the cockerel, of course, escapes. He flies up to a branch of a nearby tree and chides the wolf for his folly.

Further Latin versions of this fable such as the twelfth-century poem *Gallus et Vulpes* ('The Cock and the Fox') develop these narrative suggestions:

A hungry Fox finds a Cock crowing on his dunghill and too vigilant to be caught. So he tries flattery. 'Your father used to dance as he crew – perhaps you can't do that?' The Cock comes nearer crowing and dancing giddily. 'Why,' he asks, 'should I be thought a degenerate son?' 'Wonderful!' replies the Fox: 'your father lives again in you. But he used to shut his right eye.' 'I do the same,' says the Cock, and adds that to his performance. The Fox falls flat, overcome with admiration. 'Who would believe it? You would even excel him if you shut both eyes.' The Cock does it and is caught. Neighbours begin the chase, crying 'The Fox has got the Cock! Help, or the paragon of birds will perish!' The Fox is well away, when the Cock has a plan: 'Let my death be honourable. The pursuers say you have stolen me, and don't recognize your marvellous wit. Put me down and say "I am taking what is my own, not yours." Then I shall die happy.' The Fox carries out the suggestion and the Cock flies away. 'A plague on the unruly tongue!' cries the Fox. 'And a plague on the eyes that shut when they should see,' says the Cock.

(adapted by Kenneth Sisam)

A somewhat similar version of this story was written in the dialect of French spoken by the conquering Normans in the twelfth century. This retelling by the poet Marie de France was, she claimed, translated from an English original. If this is true – and some of Marie's commentary on her sources is suspect – it points to an already extant English version of Chaucer's story.

But there are obvious and important points of difference between the retellings we have discussed so far and Chaucer's. To be sure, *Gallus et Vulpes* provides a long religious interpretation of the story, but there is an absence of real characterization in the work. From Aesop to Marie de France the animals are essentially types – simplifications with a clear comic and didactic purpose. To find versions of the tale which humanize the animals, which give them the personality and greater imaginative range that reaches its climax in Chaucer, we have to return to France.

Somewhere around 1175 the poet Pierre de Saint Cloud made Reynard the fox the villainous hero of an animal epic. In this work – which was almost certainly modelled on the *Ysengrimus* of one Nivard, perhaps written in Ghent some thirty years previously – Reynard is involved in a series of anarchic adventures which include rape and adultery with Ysengrimus's fickle wife, and which result in Reynard's eventual trial and his escape to his castle. Such an inconclusive ending allowed for developments of the cycle by other writers. These took place with the greatest elaboration, and tales were told of Reynard's encounters with cats and crows, his disguise as a minstrel, his duels, the siege of his castle and even his funeral. These works fostered versions in German, Flemish and Italian, but the story from the Reynard cycle which particularly concerns us here is this one:

Reynard makes his way to a village in a wood, where there are many cocks and hens, geese and ducks. His special object is a favourite spot of his – the yard of a rich farmer, Constant des Noes, who is abundantly stocked with poultry, salt meat and bacon, good cherries and apples. The yard is well fenced with oak palings and thorn hurdles; and Reynard can find no way through. Yet he knows that if he jumps over, the hens will see him, and run for shelter under the thorns. At last he finds a broken paling, slips through, and hides among the cabbages. But the hens catch sight of him and run for safety.

Their flurry rouses Chantecler, who is enjoying a dust-bath in a track near the wood, and he walks proudly in, stretching his neck and trailing his wings, to inquire why they ran to the house. His favourite Pinte, 'she who laid the big eggs', replies 'We were frightened.' 'Why? What did you see?' 'Some wild beast who would harm us if we did not take shelter.' 'It's nothing, I'll swear,' said the Cock. 'Don't be afraid; you're quite safe here.' 'But I saw it this very minute,' Pinte insisted. 'Saw what?' 'I saw the fence shake and the cabbage leaves trembled where it lies.' 'Pinte,' said the Cock, 'no more of this. No fox or pole cat would dare come into this yard. A mere illusion, my dear, I assure you; so come back.' And back he went himself to his dust-bath, and there settled down, one eye open and one shut, one leg outstretched, the other doubled up.

Wearied of watching and crowing, he slept, and dreamed that there was something in the yard clad in a red fur coat fringed with bones; and it thrust the coat upon him to his great discomfort, for the collar was very tight. He starts up in terror: 'Holy Spirit,' he prays, 'save my body from prison this day and keep me safe'; and then, all his assurance gone, he runs to where the hens are hiding under the thorns and tells Pinte that he is in great dread of some wild beast or bird. 'Avoy! sweet sir,' says Pinte, 'you must not talk like that and frighten us so. By all the saints, you are a like a dog that howls before the stone hits him! Why are you so frightened?' 'I have had a strange dream,' answers the Cock, 'and an ill-omened! That is why you see me so pale. I shall tell you every detail' – (and he goes on to tell of the beast with the red fur coat). 'Do you know what it signifies?' 'Please God it turn out false!' says Pinte, 'but I can interpret it. The beast with the red fur coat is the fox; the fringe of bone is his teeth; the tight collar his mouth ... and he will get you by the neck before midday is passed. I advise you to come back, for I know he is lying in wait for you behind that clump of cabbages.' 'Pinte,' said he, 'this is folly, and it is unworthy of you to say that the beast is in this yard who shall take me by force. Curse him who believes it! for I won't believe this dream portends any harm to me.' 'God grant it may be so,' replied Pinte, 'yet if what I say is false, let me be no more your love.'

Chantecler laughs off the dream, goes back to his dust-bath, and begins to doze again. When he has settled down, Reynard creeps nearer, makes a spring, misses, and sees Chantecler jump to safety on the dunghill. Reynard is chagrined, but immediately sets his brain to work. 'Don't run away, Chantecler,' he cries, 'it is I, your own cousin.' Chantecler crows with relief. 'Do you remember your father Chanteclin?' says Reynard. 'No cock ever crew like him: one could hear him a league away when he crew with both eyes shut.' 'You are trying to trick me, cousin Reynard?' asks Chantecler. 'Indeed no! Try crowing with your eyes shut. We are one flesh and blood, and I would rather lose a paw than see you harmed.' 'I don't believe you,' says Chantecler, 'so please stand a little farther off, and I will crow for you.' 'A high note, then!' says Reynard, smiling. Chantecler crew once with one eye shut and the other open for he was suspicious of Reynard and often looked his way. 'That's nothing,' says Reynard, 'Chanteclin did not crow like that. He shut both eyes and held his note so that he could be heard twenty fields away.' Chantecler, convinced, shuts both eyes to crow. At once Reynard jumps out from under a red cabbage, seizes him by the neck, and off he goes delighted with his prize.

Pinte is beside herself with grief at the sight: 'Sir, now my warning proves true, and you laughed at me and called me a fool! Your pride was your ruin! Alas! I die of grief, for if I lose my lord I lose my honour for ever!'

The good wife opened the door, for it was evening, and called in Pinte, Rosette, and Bise, but no hen came. Then, as she called the Cock loudly, she saw Reynard going off with him and went to the rescue. Reynard increased his pace, and when she saw that she could not catch him, she gave the alarm with a full-throated 'Harro!' The farmhands ran to find out what was the matter. 'Alas!' she said, 'Disaster has come upon me.' 'How?' 'I have lost my Cock – the Fox has taken him.' 'Old slattern!' cried Constant, 'Why didn't you catch the Fox?' 'By all the saints, I couldn't.' 'Why not?' 'He wouldn't wait for me.' 'But you could hit him?' 'What with?' 'With this stick.' 'Indeed I couldn't: he ran so fast that two Breton hounds couldn't have caught him.' 'Which way?' 'That way, just there.' The farmhands ran shouting 'There he is! There he is!' Just then Reynard reached the opening and jumped down with such a thud that the pursuers heard him. 'There he is. There he is,' they cry. 'After him,' shouts Constant, and calls for his dog Nauvoisin. After him, Bardolph, Travers, Humbaut, Rebors!' They get in sight of Reynard, and shout 'There goes the Fox.'

Now Chantecler is in great peril and needs all his wit. 'Reynard,' he says, 'can't you hear the insults these men are shouting at you? When Constant shouts "Reynard has him" why not mock him by answering "In your despite"?' Reynard's cunning for once was at fault. 'In your despite!' he yelled, and as the Cock felt his jaws relax, he beat his wings and flew into an apple tree. Then he laughed at Reynard, who stood below disgusted at his own folly. 'Reynard,' he said, 'what do you think of it all?' Reynard quivered with rage: 'Cursed be the mouth,' he said, 'that makes a noise when it should be silent.' 'And,' says the Cock, 'I say a plague on the eyes that sleep when they ought to keep watch!' Then Chantecler rates Reynard for his perfidy and bids him be off before he loses his skin. Reynard runs on dejected at the loss of his dinner.

(adapted by Kenneth Sisam)

How directly did this lively story influence Chaucer? No clear answer can be given, but a number of interesting suggestions can be made. First, there are several important differences both in the narrative and the characterization of the two works. In the French version, Chauntecleer belongs to a rich male farmer called Constant des Noes. In Chaucer's version he belongs to a poor and anonymous widow. This difference is a striking one, for, as we shall see, the allegorical significance that gathers round Chaucer's Widow is of great interest and is an essential part of Chaucer's purpose. Secondly, Chaucer replaces the French Pinte with his own Pertelote, and, with far greater narrative skill, omits her first fearful glimpse of the fox and begins instead with a vivid presentation of the Widow and of Chauntecleer's voice, his astronomical accuracy, personal beauty and excessive love of his wife. In this way, Chaucer brings into prominence the main thematic motifs of his story – natural ability, pride, sex and marriage – and underscores these by developing the idea of Chauntecleer the frightened dreamer who, nonetheless, regards himself as an authority on dreams and predestination. By having Pertelote unaware of the presence of the fox, Chaucer also manages to develop a wonderfully amusing contrast between the intellectual husband and the down-to-earth, henpecking wife, whose forthright common sense is, however, inadequate to the dangers of the real world. Additionally, a particularly nice touch is that it is Pertelote rather than her husband whom Chaucer shows as dust-bathing when Chauntecleer is snatched by the fox; snatched, it should be noted, with a more ruthless speed than the French version allows for. We should further notice that by having Chauntecleer and Pertelote owned by a widow, Chaucer avoids the suggestion of marital conflict between Constant and his wife, preferring to place this in the much more suggestive context of the marriage between Chauntecleer and Pertelote themselves.

Finally we should note two factors about Chaucer's presentation of the fox. First, the eponymous hero of a large and famous tradition of French verse has, in Chaucer's version, all but lost his name. And, when he does appear, his name has been altered. He is once referred to as 'daun Russel' (l. 514), once – and this, significantly, when he is introduced – as a 'col-fox' (l. 395), but on ten other occasions he is simply termed 'the fox', 'this fox' or 'a fox'. It is as if Chaucer had deliberately depersonalized one of the most famous characters of the literature of the century before. In other words, he is concerned to emphasize the animal's status as a fox, and not his notoriety as 'Reynard'. The second and more crucial change Chaucer made to the presentation of his villain is this: in the French version, Reynard is the hero of the cycle; in Chaucer's version Russel is introduced two thirds of the way through the poem. No one can reasonably doubt that Chauntecleer is by far the more important character and that the story centres on the associations he arouses. As the Nun's Priest himself says: 'my tale is of a Cok'.

These differences between the French version and Chaucer's are significant ones, far more significant, indeed, than the few but telling verbal similarities between the works. These latter may suggest that Chaucer might have been working from an intermediate and now lost French version, but the hypothetical nature of this suggests that we could more profitably pursue other lines of inquiry.

There was a gap of nearly a hundred years between the creation of the stories in the Reynard cycle and Chaucer's poem of about 1390. This may well suggest that the French tales were somewhat old-fashioned in the minds of a fourteenth-century audience – the wealthy and the literate that is, who could afford to commission manuscripts. This does not mean that the tales had passed wholly out of circulation. Indeed, this is distinctly not the case, and in the carvings and stained glass of the greater churches – those books of the poor and the illiterate – we have a considerable quantity of evidence to suggest that the story of the cock and the fox was still a lively part of an oral culture. For example, a misericord in Ely Cathedral (a misericord is a ledge, usually carved, on the underside of a pew in a choir stall – the singer's weight could be rested on it during those parts of the service when the choir was required to stand) shows a fox preaching to a cockerel and some geese while a woman with a distaff – a figure to be identified with Chaucer's Malkin – pursues the fox who has the body of the cockerel in its jaws. Misericords in Boston, Lincolnshire, and at Beverley Minster show similar scenes, though the birds here may just be geese. Marginal illustrations in various otherwise unrelated manuscripts again show a knowledge of the stories, and similar visual evidence can be multiplied on a large scale. Thus, if the Reynard stories were somewhat old-fashioned for cultured tastes, they appear to have maintained a vigorous life among ordinary people. One very obvious reason for this is that the fox can be a destructive and expensive predator. Even today the regular appearance of one can cause considerable distress and give rise to many stories in rural areas.

But the ecclesiastical use of stories of the fox and its victims points to further matters of importance in terms of *The Nun's Priest's Tale*. These stories of the cock and the fox were rarely pure entertainment. They were often moral fables – even allegories – that could be used as the basis for teaching and sermons. In other words, these well-known stories became part of the church's resources for instructing the laity.

As we have seen, Aesop, the Latin works of the early middle ages we have mentioned, and the version of the story by Marie de France all show a clear and obvious interest in pointing a moral. In addition, a number of medieval versions of the Reynard stories developed further didactic and, more crucially, satiric material. For example, *Gallus et Vulpes* is subjected to a lengthy religious interpretation, while *Ysengrimus* contains much satire directed at the corruption of the religious orders. This is also true of the early-fourteenth-century *Renard le Contrefait*, which Chaucer appears to have known. Evidently, these widely circulated tales made a profound psychological and moral appeal to the men of the middle ages, particularly when the fox was seen as a symbol of treachery and religious hypocrisy. It was such developments as these that attracted the preachers.

The English sermon literature of the middle ages contains some of the period's most delightful prose, since in its attractiveness lay its power to convert and persuade. While many of the doctrinal issues with which the sermons deal may be abstruse and, to some modern tastes, obsessively morbid, the anecdotes with which these ideas are illustrated are often vivid and colloquial. It is these anecdotes we shall look at first. Chaucer's own Pardoner knew just how effective they could be:

> Than telle I hem ensamples many oon
> Of olde stories, longe tyme agoon:
> For lewed peple loven tales olde;
> Swich thinges can they wel reporte and holde.

lewed: unlettered, illiterate

In the words of G. R. Owst, the great authority on medieval sermons, 'We shall be fully justified . . . if . . . we lay aside the dull mass of the theological argument and concentrate solely upon these excrescences of the preaching.'

Among the most popular of the 'olde stories' or *exempla* with which skilful preachers won the 'lewed peple' in their congregations were those derived from animal lore. Behind them all lies sheer delight at the wonder and variety of God's creations, both real animals and, on many occasions, mythological ones. This delight is evident in *The Nun's Priest's Tale*. For all the complex of associations that gathers round him, Chauntecleer remains the most cockerel-like cockerel. Indeed, one critic has even gone so far as to identify his species. Chauntecleer is, we are led to believe, a Golden Spangled Hamburg. This may or may not be the case. The fact is only of passing interest – such a search for the correct species points simply to a modern preoccupation with scientific labelling and analysis. The natural history of the middle ages was concerned with wholly different matters. Though they could sometimes observe closely, the preachers were quite content to use imaginative misinformation for their purpose of drawing analogies between the behaviour of animals and the behaviour that led to the salvation or damnation of man. Here, by way of an example, is a charming piece of what seems like make-believe with which one preacher beguiled his audience:

Bartholomeus, *De proprietatibus rerum*, seys that ever betwix the eddure and the Elephaunte, be keende, is grett strive. The neddur is fowle and maliciouse, and the Elephaunte is stronge, fayre, and no-thinge grevous. The neddyr, as this clerke seyth, will com and make hym for to pleye with the elephaunte, and anon he pleys with the neddure; ffor he thenketh non ewill. But at the last this malicious worme, the neddyr, styngeth the elephaunte in the eye, as thei pley to-gethur, with his tayll. And so sodenly the eddur distrowith the elephaunte.

eddure: adder, snake   *be keende*: naturally   *distrowith*: kills

The adder, of course, represents the devil, while the elephant, so the moralization tells us, stands for the human soul. The sheer charm of such a form of instruction is irresistible. We are at once beguiled with a quaint but fascinating piece of supposed observation – note how a 'scientific' authority is cited – and led to see how it is applicable to some of the most serious issues of human life. Examples of this form of preaching can be multiplied a hundredfold. Thus, as we come to see Chauntecleer standing for – among other things – the cardinal sin of Pride, and Russel representing the devil and his snares, so we should also be aware that such a means of thought and instruction was widely popular in the period and that the Nun's Priest is drawing on a tradition wholly appropriate to his vocation.

The Nun's Priest's Tale thus uses a wide range of familiar material. Chaucer was aware of the long history of his story of the cock and the fox and reintroduced it into the major literature of his time in a way that highlights his particular interests and shows his sense of comic narrative. He also knew that the tale had a wide circulation in the church and drew on a range of sermon techniques further to develop his ideas. It is wholly appropriate that a story fashioned in this way should be given to the Nun's Priest, since it was the responsibility of men so licensed to preach and maintain moral and religious standards. To appreciate this more fully we should now turn to examine the teller of the Tale himself.

3. The Nun's Priest

We have noted the pervasive influence of the church on *The Canterbury Tales*. Many of the pilgrims are professionals within it and all are more or less united by the ideals of pilgrimage itself. *The General Prologue* vividly establishes the presence of most of them, but the teller of our particular tale emerges there merely as the appendage of a great lady. The Prioress, we are told, was accompanied by another nun 'and preestes three'. These men enhanced her status, afforded her some measure of protection, and attended to her spiritual needs – as a woman the Prioress was not permitted to preach or minister the sacraments – but all we are told about them for the present suggests that these commonplace figures of medieval life are as alike as peas in a pod.

The teller of our particular tale emerges as a character at a most interesting and critical moment. The Monk has been wearying the company with his dreary, mechanical list of catastrophes that befell the great and the famous. This was one of the conventional forms or genres of medieval literature. It was known on the Continent and was further exploited in England by Lydgate – one of Chaucer's most devoted imitators – in his *Fall of Princes*, a poem that manages to stretch to some 36,000 lines. The tedium of the genre is self-evident and was obviously felt even by contemporaries. The Knight, for example, whom Chaucer presents as the flower of courtesy, a man who has never said anything unbecoming in all his life, nonetheless feels impelled to ask the Monk to cease his recital. Such repetitious gloom is not for him. Nor does it appeal to the vigorously extrovert Harry Bailey. With gusty colloquial vigour, the rough spontaneity of an ordinary man of the world, Harry Bailey launches an attack on the Monk which reads like a release of pent-up frustration. He satirizes the Monk's language, is repelled by the idea of 'Tragedie' inherent in the Monk's use of the 'Fall of Princes' genre, and agrees with the Knight that it is no good crying over spilt milk. In short, the Monk's tale offers no entertainment, no 'desport ne game'. Harry Bailey is, he says, fully able to understand and appreciate a well-told tale – a point of some significance – but the Monk's lack of artistry has lost him his audience. As the Host adds, it is only the clinking of the bells of the Monk's bridle that has stopped him from going to sleep and falling off his horse.

This last is a vivid touch, but it is also rather more than this and its full significance introduces us to some ways of thought that are important to our interpretation of medieval works of literature in general, to our understanding of the Monk himself and hence to the context in which *The Nun's Priest's Tale* should be read. Thus, while falling from one's horse may have been a real physical risk to be made the subject of a joke, it was also a conventional image of the fall of Pride – the very subject of the Monk's tale. However, Harry Bailey uses the image – whether knowingly or not – as a means of making clear the extreme boredom the Monk's tale induces in him. In other words, it is a neatly ironic way of pointing out the Monk's artistic failure.

But there is also rather more here than an implied satire on bad story-telling and preaching. The bells are an image of the Monk's moral weakness. They are loud and showy. They are part of the sumptuous equipment he lavishes on one of his favourite occupations: horses and hunting. In *The General Prologue* we are told that the Monk is a strong, vigorously physical man, competent and, above all, worldly. He rejects the old, strict rules of the monastic life. He needs to live out in the world, not walled away from it. As a result, he is expensively dressed, bright eyed and 'a lord full fat and in good point'. In addition to the bells on his bridle, he has an excellent stable of horses, a pack of greyhounds with which he goes hunting hares and a gourmet's love of roast swan. And, just as Harry

Bailey's image of falling from his horse carries implications a modern reader might miss, so these details are also a special aspect of Chaucer's moral interest in the Monk. We shall discuss them here so that we may have some idea of the contrast Chaucer draws between this worldly prelate and the humble Nun's Priest.

The horses and the bells suggest the Monk's worldliness on a number of levels. First his palfrey – a spirited mount also favoured by the Prioress – was a popular *cheval de parade* with knights and ladies, and probably had the class associations about it we now associate with certain makes of cars. Taken together with the hunting of hares – considered an aristocratic pastime when compared to snaring rabbits – and the Monk's expensive hounds, we are offered here a picture whose moral significance is explained by Wycliffe: 'prestis wasting in othere thingis, as ben horsis, haukis & houndes ... ben ful dampnable bifore god', wrote the zealous reformer. And this sense of damnation is enhanced by the conventional associations of hares with lechery and the possible but obvious sexual symbolism suggested by riding – 'ryde' is the verb used by Chauntecleer to express coitus – a suggestion furthered by the Monk's sporting a gold brooch with an elaborate love-knot on it. This makes it clear that he has broken his vow of chastity. We might also bear in mind here the medieval idea of the worldly hunter, exulting in the physical world, suggested by his horse, becoming himself the quarry of fiends and hell-hounds. Finally, the bells and ornaments that adorn the Monk's horse are an indication not just of an extrovert worldliness but of the cardinal sin of Pride. The Parson – Chaucer's model cleric – makes this clear in his sermon on confession and the Seven Deadly Sins:

I sey nat that honestetee in clothinge of man or womman is uncovenable, but certes the superfluitee or disordinat scantitee of clothinge is reprevable. Also the sinne of adornement or of apparaille is in thinges that apertenen to rydinge, as in to manye delicat horses that been holden for delyt, that been so faire, fatte, and costlewe; and also to many a vicious knave that is sustened by cause of hem; in to curious harneys, as in sadeles, in crouperes, peytrels, and brydles covered with precious clothing and riche, barres and plates of gold and of silver. For which god seith by Zakarie the prophete, 'I wol confounde the ryderes of swiche horses.' This folk taken litel reward of the rydinge of goddes sone of hevene, and of his harneys whan he rood up-on the asse, and ne hadde noon other harneys but the povre clothes of hise disciples; ne we ne rede nat that evere he rood on other beest.

unconvenable: unseemly *disordinat*: wrongful
reprevable: reprehensible *peytrels*: breast-piece of harness
reward: have regard

Pride, of course, is the chief of the Seven Deadly Sins and it is one of the ironies that Chaucer most effectively exploits in the *The Canterbury Tales* that many of the narratives tell us much about the moral stature of those who tell them. *The Pardoner's Tale* for example, is a most vigorous sermon against the sin of Avarice, another of the Deadly Sins. The Pardoner takes as his text the motto *radix malorum est cupiditas* – 'the love of money is the root of all evil'. It is precisely the love of money that is the driving trait of the Pardoner's own bizarre character. Like the Monk, he preaches against the abuses he most fully personifies. However, unlike the Monk, who informs us that he has upwards of a hundred of the sort of 'tragedies' he recites in his cell, the Pardoner is a great and engaging artist. The pride of the Monk, on the other hand, makes him a pompous bore, a man trapped in the vices against which he so ineffectively preaches.

When Harry Bailey turns from the Monk who, understandably enough, has retreated into silence after the onslaught on his tale, our impression of the Nun's Priest begins to fill out. We learn, for instance, that far from being mounted on an expensive palfrey, the Nun's Priest has to make do with a horse that is 'bothe foule and lene'. In other words, the man is poor, the ill-provided servant of a great lady of the church. We should also notice his humble willingness to tell his tale and should perhaps detect a quiet, engaging humour in his promise to be 'mery'. We have just seen Harry Bailey at his most overbearing ridiculing the Monk for the boredom and depression that his tale induces. The Nun's Priest's wry assessment of this suggests a certain tact and intelligence on his part. Finally, to complete our initial impression and reinforce the contrast to the Monk, Chaucer calls the Nun's Priest 'this swete preest, this goodly man, Sir John'. In other words, poor and apparently reserved though he seems, we are told that the Nun's Priest is a fine individual who admirably fulfils the requirements of his vocation.

The Nun's Priest's status as a literary device

We have characterized the Nun's Priest in contrast to the Monk as the poor, perhaps rather downtrodden, servant of a great lady of the church, a man of some tact, blessed with an alert but gentle sense of irony, whom Chaucer clearly regarded as both a creditable member of his vocation and a worthy individual. However, what this introduction does not prepare us for is the fact that *The Nun's Priest's Tale* is one of the great comic masterpieces of English literature, a poem that is not simply funny, but learned, serious and very shrewd. Where the Monk bores the company with his dreary recitation of instances exemplifying the fall of Pride, the

Nun's Priest, taking up the same theme, tells a tale which is hugely engaging, stylistically various, and weaves dexterously together some of the most serious intellectual issues of the day. It does this in a manner that, far from exulting in fashionable new insights – and so falling into the error of intellectual pride – reveals a wryly mature and agile mind illuminated by that great gift – humour.

Clearly, these intellectual qualities of the Tale are a central part of the teller's character, but before we can assess them we need to have some idea of the intellectual milieu with which the Nun's Priest shows an acquaintance. To achieve this, we shall have to discuss his supposed relation to the following areas: education both at school and in the universities, biblical, theological and philosophical training, the skills required of preachers, and something of the popular tenor of religious life. When we have some purchase on such matters, when we have seen them as the medieval equivalents of our own intellectual concerns, then we shall be able to appreciate the Nun's Priest's wide knowledge of contemporary issues which allowed him to review many of these things in a kindly, wry and detached way. These qualities are all essential aspects of his presentation.

But first a word of warning: what follows is not an attempt to trace the supposed career of a real individual. The Nun's Priest is a creation of Chaucer's art. He has no existence outside the text of the poem. He is purely Chaucer the poet's vehicle for a particular form of comic wisdom. But that wisdom operates on some of the major issues of the day, and these *are* matters of historical fact. They need to be put in their historical setting. Only when we have done this can we appreciate the qualities of mind revealed by Chaucer's imaginary creation. Thus, although we shall be looking at such matters as who was interested in issues of free will in medieval England and glancing at private libraries, university theology and conventional aspects of the training of a priest, we should not assume that the Nun's Priest himself had such a library or went up to Oxford to be influenced by such and such a teacher. We can know nothing more about the Nun's Priest than the text tells us – and what the text tells us is that this fictional creation, this all but anonymous priest, is Chaucer's means of showing particular qualities of response to certain current issues. Many of these issues, as we shall see, were dependent on the far from universal skill of literacy.

Some aspects of literacy in medieval England

The Nun's Priest reveals himself as a man of extensive learning. Education in fourteenth-century English schools revolved mainly around Latin grammar and the teaching of Latin literature. The reason for this was simple enough. Latin was the international language of European culture, of its traditions and its great medieval institution the church. While English and – far more extensively – French had their vernacular literatures, Latin was the common language of European thought; the language of major theology, philosophy and much poetry. This sense of tradition is emphasized by the fact that competence in Latin was often instilled – more or less effectively – by the local vicar from standard texts that had survived from the late Roman period. By the time of the composition of *The Nun's Priest's Tale*, oral instruction in Latin grammar was largely conducted in English rather than French. Access to schools – which were run by the church – was relatively open, particularly after teaching posts became endowed rather than dependent on fees. And the effects of this were significant. While some scholars would have gone on to become priests, there remained a considerable number who swelled the ranks of the literate laity. Such men would have had at least a functional acquaintance with Latin. Chaucer himself was certainly one such, but Chauntecleer, who in some respects stands for this class of educated men, considers himself rather more than functionally proficient in Latin. Nonetheless, his alleged skills crucially fail him.

Relatively few men went on to university – women, of course, had no place in the great academic institutions – but the influence of university ideas was out of all proportion to the numbers that received higher education. The Nun's Priest is clearly familiar with the issues debated. In addition to the teaching offered in grammar, letter-writing and the skills required for administration, the more accessible of the university's philosophical and theological ideas were disseminated through the pulpit – an institution whose power to persuade and inform it is now difficult to recapture – while cathedrals also arranged for theological lectures to be given by university figures, thereby further educating the literate laity. It is thus clear that there was a reasonably wide public moderately well informed about such matters as fortune and free will, which the Nun's Priest discusses, a public whose members included at least some whose interest and literacy extended far enough to read the translations of Boethius and other thinkers made by Chaucer and his contemporaries. Indeed, translation in such areas was a productive aspect of English literature during the period, and this, added to the idea that *The Canterbury Tales* was early perceived and presented as a compilation of wisdom, suggests that the issues discussed by the Nun's Priest were far from arcane.

We can thus begin to characterize the Nun's Priest as an educated, literate man, well versed in popular contemporary issues and able to communicate them effectively. These were important qualities at a time when complaints about the ignorance of the clergy were widespread. Chaucer himself, as we have seen, was quick enough to point out clerical abuses, but it is essential to realize that he also had a profound reverence for the traditional teaching of the church when it was honestly practised. We have seen that in *The Canterbury Tales* he describes the Nun's Priest as 'sweet' – a man perfectly adjusted to his vocation – and in his portrait of the Parson in *The General Prologue* we learn more of the particular qualities Chaucer admired in such men: personal integrity and devotion, unpretentious, hard-working charity, a willingness to teach, an ease with all sorts and conditions of people, and a faith founded on the Bible and traditional doctrine. We are told that the Parson was 'of holy thoght and werk', that he was a 'lerned' man, a devout preacher and teacher, loyal to parishioners, patient of his poverty, while, above all:

> ... Cristes lore, and his apostles twelve,
> He taughte, but first he fol it himselve.

This way of life was an ideal, of course, but it is interesting to compare these much admired qualities to those shown by the Nun's Priest – in particular his ability to preach what we can partly classify as an engaging sermon based on faith and wide learning.

Some aspects of the Nun's Priest's knowledge and training: sermons, animal imagery, the Seven Deadly Sins, medieval philosophy and theology

(i) SERMONS

Preaching was a matter of the greatest importance to the culture of the middle ages. St Thomas Aquinas, the man who gave definitive form to the theology of the Catholic church, called it 'the noblest of all the ecclesiastical functions', and declared that preachers are 'the mouth of Christ'. And it is from the New Testament that medieval traditions of preaching largely stem.

The synoptic gospels place great emphasis on Christ's ordering his disciples to preach and on portraying Christ himself as a model for this. For example, Christ used both direct instruction and, more relevant to our immediate concern, parables. As a fourteenth-century English cleric declared, 'In various parables and examples he instigated the people, both Jewish and Christian, to abstain from vices and pursue virtues. And this is what he said in Mark iv, 2 – "He taught them many things in parables."' The forty major parables of the synoptic gospels are accompanied by a statement of the moral lesson each contains, and the use of such a technique is made clear in Mark iv, 33–4: 'in many such parables he spoke the word to them, according as they were able to understand it; but without a parable he did not speak to them. But privately he explained all things to his disciples.' This idea of a simple story that appealed to the crowd but which, nonetheless, contained a more abstruse teaching for the better-informed, is central to much sermon theory in the middle ages and bears obvious analogies to the delightful narrative and deeper allegorical concerns of *The Nun's Priest's Tale*. Lastly, Christ's particular use of parables – that of the Lost Sheep, for example – gave huge importance to the idea that the visible universe – in this case the world of animals – can be read as an analogy of divine truth. Just as the Lost Sheep represents the erring, so a cockerel could stand for the proud. The physical universe could thus be seen as a book which the learned could interpret for its ethical and religious significance. We shall return to this in a moment, but already it is possible to see the giving of such sermons as we expect to find in *The Nun's Priest's Tale* as a continuation of the earliest Christian practice, and the preacher himself, as he performs his function, in certain respects imitating Christ.

Such an exalted concept of preaching and instruction clearly placed huge responsibilities on the preacher. He needed considerable knowledge, skill in communication and the clear personal rectitude that would inspire respect. Ideally these qualities were merged, and it will be useful if we consider them here in relation to a definition of preaching itself.

The twelfth-century writer Alain de Lille regarded preaching as one of the highest activities of the Christian life and the one which revealed 'the perfection of the whole man'. Preaching could only be pursued competently by one who was already disciplined by confession, prayer and study. So prepared, he could perform his task which Alain defined thus: 'Preaching is an open and public instruction in faith and morals, zealously serving the information of mankind, proceeding by the narrow path of reason and growing from the spring of the sacred text.' Alain elaborates on this by explaining that preaching must be open and public so that it does not seem to smack of heresy and because it is for the benefit of many people, giving clear information about theological issues and, just as pertinently to our story, instruction on the proper conduct of life. Preaching should also be interesting but sober in style and draw from the Bible and received teaching. *The Nun's Priest's Tale* clearly fulfils many of these requirements, and we shall go on to examine in more detail its precise and often ironic relation to the rhetorical skills preachers were required to possess. However, since our immediate purpose is to try and elucidate some of the characteristics of Chaucer's Nun's Priest himself, it will be more useful if we concentrate here on the personal requirements generally expected of a preacher charged with the great responsibility of leading souls to salvation. It is such conventional expectations as these against which we can then measure the Nun's Priest's character as Chaucer initially presents it and so clarify the impact he might have been expected to make on his contemporaries.

Since sermons were regarded as a medicine 'by which the disease of sin is purged' and were intended to rouse the soul from languor and recall it to a life of virtue, it was necessary that the preacher himself be both a man of moral rectitude and lovable in his own right. It was thus recognized that the personal strengths of the preacher were an important part of his effectiveness. It is at once obvious how the erring and disdainful Monk lacks these qualities. By way of contrast, the proper attitude of a preacher, declared one writer, should be 'good will, devout love, and a clear conscience'. A preacher's interior struggles will have taught him 'to act wisely for his own salvation and that of others'. But such personal knowledge is not in itself enough. Deep learning is also essential to effective preaching. 'It is extremely dangerous for a man who has the obligation of preaching ever to stop studying,' declared the writer of one manual on how sermons should be given, but the same authority stated that the intellectual pride that may well go with scholarship should be zealously avoided. He warns the would-be preacher against striving to deal with the more difficult passages of Scripture and enunciating 'grave platitudes in carefully polished phrases, not in order to help his hearers live better, but to feed his own ego by demonstrating that he knows more'. Further, the good and humble preacher should arrange and deliver his matter clearly and, above all, avoid tedium and excessive length. St Ambrose declared that a tedious sermon arouses anger, but the Monk has clearly forgotten this truth, as the reactions of his bored audience illustrate. The Monk's exhortation to virtue fails because he himself lacks both virtue and technical skill. The Nun's Priest, on the other hand, shows – at first, at least – many of the strengths conventionally required of the good preacher. Chaucer makes clear at the start that he is an attractive man and this is important since, in the words of St Gregory: 'It is indeed difficult for a preacher who is not loved ... to be willingly listened to.' In addition to his attractive manner, the Nun's Priest also shows a willingness to preach, which was not always apparent in others. It was recognized, in the words of one writer, that 'some refuse to do it out of pride, some out of laziness, and some out of envy'. The teller of our particular tale accepts his role with readiness.

The Nun's Priest thus reveals a becoming humility, a genuine knowledge of the issues he discusses, great technical ability and the loving concern that allows him to tell a tale of interest both to the intellectuals in the party and to the less educated. This he achieves by telling a delightful beast fable capable of many levels of interpretation. We should now examine something of the background to this. Again, such matters are an important aspect of the Nun's Priest's training.

(ii) ANIMAL IMAGERY

We have seen that it was widely believed that animal stories appealed to all members of the laity and that such exempla were frequently taken from natural history.

Why? The most obvious reason – and the one that partly accounts for the fact that beast fables are found in all cultures and at all times – is the fact that however far we may be dependent on animals for food, the degree of affection that they arouse is naturally seen in anthropomorphic terms. In other words, we relate animals' reactions to human reactions. This is the fundamental imaginative appeal of *The Nun's Priest's Tale.* Chauntecleer is at once a most cockerel-like cockerel and a most engaging personality. But there is far more to it than this. Charm and intuitive sympathy – what we may call the *Tom and Jerry* element – are indeed of the utmost importance to *The Nun's Priest's Tale,* but they are not in themselves enough. Fully to appreciate why the Nun's Priest and other preachers regarded animals as fit vehicles for moral instruction we must make a further journey into the medieval mind. When we have completed it we shall be in a better position to appreciate both the seriousness of Chaucer's beast fable and its wise comedy.

'All creation, like a book or a picture, is a mirror to us – a true figure of our life, our death, our condition, our lot.' So wrote Alain de Lille. Behind his obscure statement lies the profound and all-embracing faith of the Catholic middle ages. It tells us that the world was not created by some cosmic accident – a 'big bang' perhaps; that monsters – which the medieval imagination had in plenty – did not develop out of the protozoic slime to be replaced after millennia by more effective species. Rather, it tells us that the idea of the world as it now is was present in the mind of God from the beginning, that he created it, and that in all its aspects – animal, vegetable, mineral and human – it is a vast and ever-changing symbol of his divine thought and purposes. Nature must be read in the light of faith. True knowledge is not scientific knowledge, the dividing of animals into species and thinking we have done what we can when we have specified a hen as the type Golden Spangled Hamburg, which may or may not be an efficient producer of eggs. This is the sort of knowledge that leads only to the battery farm. As we have seen, the medieval view required that nature be read as an image of God and his mercy towards man. It is a divine allegory. Whatever his particular breed, whatever his functional efficiency, Chauntecleer should not be seen simply as a particular animal with a particular 'character', but as a symbolic representation of the virtues and vices that define man's relationship to his maker. In particular, Chauntecleer personifies the chief of the vices, Pride, and the primal sin that led to man's fall, uxoriousness, the placing of married love before reason and faith.

We are thus moving in a world of symbols and allegory. To get a surer understanding of why animals could represent ethical and religious truths in this way we should now turn to examine something that lies at the heart of the middle ages: its allegorical reading of the Bible. When we have done so, we will be able to see how the world of animals, allegorically conceived, was at one with the word of God when allegorically interpreted.

The early middle ages inherited a wide curriculum of studies from the ancient world that, through the labours of the great doctors of the church, was absorbed into Christian doctrine and knowledge. Natural history of a sort was part of this and all subjects had their place in the great task of interpreting the Bible. That act of interpretation, as we have mentioned, was of a particular kind. Far from the modern emphasis on history, archaeology and the scientific study of authorship and authenticity, the medieval Bible – which contained many sections we now wholly reject – was considered the absolute word of God, which could be interpreted in its literal or historical sense – in other words for its straightforward narrative meaning. Secondly – and for our purposes more crucially – it could also be read in an allegorical sense. Thirdly, a tropological interpretation pointed out the moral of a particular incident and related this to faith and doctrine, both of which were strengthened thereby. Finally, a fourth sense – the anagogical – allowed biblical events to be seen as an image of the soul's often mystic relation to God. Here is how one medieval scholar described the technique:

There are four ways of interpreting Scripture; on them, as though on so many scrolls, each sacred page is rolled. The first is History, which speaks of actual events as they occurred; the second is Allegory, in which one thing stands for something else; the third is Tropology, or moral instruction, which treats of the ordering and arranging of one's life; and the last is Anagogy, or spiritual enlightenment, through which we who are about to treat of heavenly and lofty topics are led to a higher way of life For example, the word 'Jerusalem': historically it represents a specific city; in allegory it represents the holy Church; tropologically, or morally, it is the soul of every faithful man who longs for the vision of eternal peace; and anagogically it refers to the life of the heavenly citizens, who already see the God of Gods, revealed in all his glory in Sion. Granted that all four of these methods of interpretation are valid and can be used, either together or singly, yet the most appropriate and prudent for use in matters referring to the lives of men seems to be the moral approach.

This is a way of reading a text that we have now almost totally abandoned. And yet it is of the greatest historical importance. It is the means by which men and women understood both the Bible and much of their poetry for a millennium and a half. We should try to understand it in our turn. We should recognize that it would have been thoroughly familiar – indeed, obvious – to many members of Chaucer's audience, not least to the Nun's Priest with his theological training. When we have come to appreciate it, we shall see that his delightful story of the cock and the fox, taken at face value, provides us with the historical sense, its allegorical intention is also clear, while its tropological or moral sense – its analysis of Pride and related sins – make up an important part both of its intellectual core and of the profit that a medieval audience would have derived from it. As another medieval scholar declared, 'When the nature of sin is clearly recognized, its opposite, the nature of virtue, will be known with equal clarity, as grain is clearly distinguished from chaff.'

All of man's intellectual knowledge could be brought to bear on interpreting the Bible in this fourfold way. Hence the interest in animals, plants, number symbolism, astrology and music. These were not ends in themselves – ways of controlling nature for man's benefit and power – but sciences in the service of God which led hopefully to man's salvation. By looking at animals as symbolic representations of the teaching of the Bible – by viewing a lost sheep as an erring soul, for example – the ordinary natural world led the inquirer further into scriptural truth, and, as St Augustine maintained, enchanted him into faith. In the following passage, St Augustine contrasts the ineffectiveness of bald scriptural exposition with the delight of the sort of allegorical interpretation we have been talking about. He thereby defines both the means and the power of such ways of thought:

Why is there less pleasure in hearing that the Saints are men, by whose life and example the Church of Christ strips those who come to her of false doctrines, and receives into her body those who imitate their virtues, and that these faithful and true servants of God, laying aside the weight of secular affairs, come to the cleansing of baptism and arise thence informed by the Holy Spirit to bring forth the fruit of a two-fold charity towards God and their neighbour – why is this less pleasurable than to hear the exposition of that sentence in the Song of Songs where it is said of the Church as of a beautiful woman, *Thy teeth are like a flock of sheep that are newly shorn, which come up from the washing, whereof every one bears twins, and none is barren among them*? A man learns nothing from this which he might not learn from the plainest words spoken without the aid of allegory. Yet (I know not why) I find it more sweet to think of the Saints as the teeth of the Church, separating men from their errors and passing them as it were softened and masticated into the body of the Church. And I find an immense sweetness in thinking of the shorn sheep, laying aside secular burdens – as it were their fleece – and coming from the dip, which is baptism, each bringing forth two lambs – the double law of charity – and none being sterile among them.

This is theology in its guise as agricultural science. Sheep farming acts as an allegory of salvation. In *The Nun's Priest's Tale*, the Widow's little dairy enterprise likewise becomes an allegory of some of the principal vices that lead man's soul into peril.

The facts – or alleged facts – about animals that were pressed into the service of religion derived from a number of sources. The nature of these will enable us to see further into the theological forms of medieval natural history.

Among the works of Aristotle inherited by the middle ages was his *Historia animalum*. While Aristotle can be seen as the founder of scientific zoology, a man whose influence reigned for eighteen centuries, his work contains much popular animal lore and even citations from Aesop – a source of animal wisdom whose influence on the middle ages we have already discussed. The Roman Pliny repeated much of what he found in Aristotle, and, while all these works had their part to play, medieval writers could also draw on other sources. From the Bible, for example, they would have learnt of the cunning of the fox – Judges xv, 4–5, Song of Solomon ii, 15, Luke xiii, 32 – while a handful of works derive in varying degrees from one of the most curious and influential of all such books, the *Physiologus*, a work probably dating from the second century and of Greek origin. Although declared heretical, the *Physiologus* was widely translated and hugely influential. It is even cited in *The Nun's Priest's Tale* itself (l. 451). What made it particularly attractive were the allegories added to it by a Christian writer. For example, expanding on the idea that wasps can be suffocated in oil, the analogy that sprang naturally to the commentator's mind was the devil who can be destroyed by the oil of good works. In this particular case, some additional sentences reveal exactly the world we are discussing. Having drawn his analogy between wasps and the devil, the writer asks:

What spiritual truth do we learn from this? For this has not been ordered foolishly by the Creator of all things, but has been ordained for our instruction

– all this the great and the small, so that, when we consider the things visible to us, we are undertaking the knowledge of the invisible. For we, in our bodies as we now are, cannot attain the invisible except through the visible. For that which cannot be seen by reason of the dullness of our bodies is pictured to us as it were through a form or image of Him who cares for all things which by Him were brought into being

Such a way of thought again suggests how we can see the abundantly physical Chauntecleer as a personification of invisible moral qualities such as Pride and uxoriousness. Like the drowning wasps, he helps in our moral education.

Here then was a basis for some of the most elaborate examples of sanctified natural history. The interpretation by allegory that was brought to the Bible – the book of God's word – could also be brought to nature – the book of his creation. All living things could magnify the Lord; and, as the *Physiologus* was expanded, illuminated and circulated, so some of the most delightful books of the middle ages – the Bestiaries – gave ever greater prominence to this sacred folk-lore. As we shall see, the relationship of both Russel and Chauntecleer to many of these works is evident, and we shall have to return to such matters later.

Though nature could now be interpreted as an image of humanity in its relation to God, a crucial difference existed between the order of brute creation and that of man. Briefly put, man has a soul and therefore immortal longings and responsibilities, while animals do not. This aspect of the matter particularly interested Chaucer. In *The Knight's Tale*, for example, one of the imprisoned heroes laments that while animals may do whatever they like without fear of punishment in an afterlife, man, suffering already in his limited earthly existence, must behave himself or – such is divine mercy – suffer an eternity of pain for finite sins:

> And yet encreseth this all my penaunce,
> That man is bounden to his observaunce,
> For Goddes sake, to letten of his wille,
> Ther as a beest may al his lust fulfille.
> And whan a beest is deed, he hath no peyne;
> But man after his deeth moot wepe and pleyne,
> Though in this world he have care and wo;
> With-outen doute it may stonden so.

> *penaunce*: torment   *observaunce*: set duty
> *letten*: restrain

Animals, because they have no souls, can do as they wish, while man must live in accordance with a moral law. And it is just this latter that gives man his spiritual dignity. Through the exercise of virtue he can rise above brute creation. If he relaxes his efforts, however, he falls to the level of beasts. Animals can thus become effective symbols of the depths to which man can sink. They can represent him at his most sinful. This idea may be found in one of Chaucer's most revered sources, *The Consolation of Philosophy* by Boethius. Here is the relevant passage in Chaucer's own translation:

> Thanne bitydeth it, that yif thou seest a wight that be transformed into vyces, thou ne mayst nat wene that he be a man.
>
> For yif he be ardaunt in avaryce, and that he be a ravinour by violence of foreine richesse, thou shalt seyn that he is lyke to the wolf. And yif he be felonous and with-oute reste, and exercyse his tonge to chydinges thou shalt lykne him to the hound. And yif he be a prevey awaitour y-hid, and reioyseth him to ravisshe by wyles, thou shalt seyn him lyke to the fox-whelpes. And yif he be distempre and quaketh for ire, men shal wene that he bereth the corage of a lyoun. And yif he be dredful and fleinge, and dredeth thinges that ne oughten nat to ben dred, men shal holden him lyk to the hert. And yif he be slow and astoned and lache, he liveth as an asse. And yif he be light and unstedefast of corage, and chaungeth ay his studies, he is lykned to briddes. And if he be plounged in foule and unclene luxuries, he is with-holden in the foule delyces of the foule sowe. Thanne folweth it, that he that forleteth bountee and prowesse, he forleteth to ben a man; sin he may nat passen in-to the condicioun of god, he is torned in-to a beest.

wight: person   *wene*: believe   *ravinour*: plunderer   *prevey awaitour y-hid*: one who lies hidden and secretly in wait   *wyles*: tricks   *distempre*: angry   *corage*: heart   *dredful*: fearful   *astoned*: stupid   *lache*: lazy, dull   *delyces*: delights   *bountee*: virtue   *forleteth*: ceases

Sinful man falls to the level of beasts and beasts symbolize the Seven Deadly Sins. Since these provide a crucial vocabulary of analysis for *The Nun's Priest's Tale*, let us examine them in more detail.

(iii) THE SEVEN DEADLY SINS

The most widely accepted hierarchy of the Seven Deadly Sins was that suggested by Gregory the Great in the late sixth century and which, in one of its most common forms, placed Pride as the root of Wrath, Envy, Avarice, Sloth, Gluttony and Luxury. This is the list and – substantially – the order, that Chaucer himself adopted when he included a treatise on the Sins in *The Parson's Tale*. We shall make frequent reference to this when we consider the character of Chauntecleer, but should concentrate here on the background to the Sins, their nature, and the many sources of their dissemination which led to their being both a natural medium of analysis to the Nun's Priest and matters of commonplace knowledge to his audience.

The idea of listing sins is an ancient one and strong traces of our list and the seven items it contains can be found in the declining classical world that also gave birth to the *Physiologus*. The list was particularly developed by early Christian ascetics meditating on the nature of sin in the wastelands of the Egyptian desert and was brought to the West in the fifth century. The Seven Deadly Sins were then incorporated into Catholic theology by Gregory the Great and thereafter spread rapidly through Christendom.

St Thomas Aquinas considered the Sins to be among the final causes which give rise to all the other sins of humankind. As the Parson declares: 'been they cleped chieftaines for-as-muche as they been chief, and springers of alle othere sinnes'. They are the fundamental errors which pervert the will away from what the intellect knows to be man's proper good and incline it instead to something which only appears to be good – worldly pride or sexual indulgence, for example – which is in fact sinful because it places earthly pleasure before obedience to God.

Since sin is a rather unfashionable concept today, it may be helpful if we examine the medieval conception of it more fully. In so doing, we shall get closer to the ethical universe of the Nun's Priest and his Tale concerning – among others – the sin of Pride.

Sin is incumbent on all men – the children of Adam – because of the Fall. The familiar Genesis story tells how the devil, disguised as a serpent, tempted Eve to eat an apple from the Tree of Knowledge which God had forbidden both her and Adam to touch. In the Parson's words: 'The womman thanne saugh that the tree was good to feding, and fair to the eyen, and delytable to the sighte; she tok of the fruit of the tree, and eet it, and yaf [gave] to hir housbonde, and he eet.' It should be noticed that Eve has been tempted purely through her senses. The apples looked good to her and she wanted to eat one. She yielded to 'the delyt of the flesh'. Adam, however, created by God as a being superior in intellect to Eve, was not so simply won. He did not fall through simple greed but, by deliberately placing love of his wife before loving obedience to God, made a conscious decision to eat the apple, join with Eve, and so fall through a perversion of his intellect and his will. Thus interpreted, the Genesis story shows sin as the devil's first prompting fleshly appetite and then overcoming reason and the will and turning them from God. This is the model for all subsequent temptations of mankind who, as Adam's children, have inherited a natural propensity to sin which leads inevitably to death. As the Parson says, 'of thilke Adam toke we thilke sinne original;

for of him fleshly descended be we alle, and engendered of vile and corrupt matere'.

It is particularly interesting to note here how Chauntecleer, overcome like the original Adam with love of his wife, forgets his intellectual self and the warnings he has interpreted from his dream and, in his desire for sex, falls into mortal danger. We have already mentioned that there was a strongly marked tendency in the middle ages to draw analogies between the Bible and man's contemporary life in the world, and to this idea of Chauntecleer as a parallel or 'type' of Adam we shall return.

Each man's inheritance of original sin predisposes him to all manner of sinful behaviour. The concept of the Seven Deadly Sins gave a popular and effective means both of analysing this and of showing the relationships between the Sins. It was particularly appropriate that since the original fall of man centred on a tree, so the Seven Deadly Sins themselves were conventionally seen as springing from the root of Pride, while, as Chaucer's Parson declares: 'everich of thise chief sinnes hath hise braunches and hise twigges'. Interconnections as close as this suggest that a man committing one of the Deadly Sins may easily be led into committing more, and we shall see that Chauntecleer's Pride and uxorious Lust lead him into a considerable range of error. Again, the list provided by the Seven Deadly Sins will help us towards enumerating these.

However, we should look first at the ways by which the concept of the Seven Deadly Sins was disseminated. We shall find that the list was indeed widely circulated and that considerable efforts were made to instruct the laity in it. For example, a council at Lambeth in 1281 ruled, under instruction from the papacy, that priests should instruct their congregations in the Sins, and the same order was repeated at the Synod of Ely in 1364. As a result, a large number of works of instruction were written to help priests carry out this function. Similar in purpose were the handbooks on preaching and collections of exemplary stories that were again written in large numbers for the purpose of instructing the laity, often with, at their core, the concept of the Seven Deadly Sins. For example, the *Summa praedicantium*, by the Cambridge Dominican John Bromyard – and the Dominicans and Franciscans were particularly important in the huge rise of popular preaching in the thirteenth and fourteenth centuries – is an elaborate reference work, arranged under topic headings and supplemented with a collection of exemplary stories, sacred and profane, arranged to relate to alphabetically presented articles which include material on the Sins. Such works as these allowed preachers to gather together a great range of material relevant to their themes and interests. Further, these and similar works of commentary had a great appeal to the literate laity, and we shall see that Chaucer actually used one of them – a commentary on the biblical 'Wisdom' literature by Robert Holcot – as his source for Chauntecleer's knowledge of dreams and dreamlore.

The purpose behind this wide dissemination of material on the Seven Deadly Sins was a deeply serious one: the salvation of man's soul by his recognition of his errors, and his subsequent penitence, confession and making satisfaction. These matters were naturally of the greatest moment and were a crucial part of the sacramental office of the church by which the sinner could, through the sacrifice of Christ, be forgiven his errors and so prepared for an afterlife of bliss. Failure to achieve this state led to damnation or purgatory: 'the horrible peynes of helle'. Yet, while this terrifying element of eternal damnation could never be forgotten in an age that interpreted all experience in terms of religion, we should not forget the great skill and artistry – the sheer delight – that was often brought to the presentation of the Seven Deadly Sins themselves. Satire and exemplary stories had their part to play in this and the Sins became an important part of the popular imagination, as the Nun's Priest well knew. Indeed, in the words of Morton W. Bloomfield:

> The preachers ... used the cardinal sins very often in their messages to the people; and it would be hard to exaggerate their influence in popularizing the concept. In fact, they and the confessors impressed the cardinal sins so deeply on the popular mind that the Sins came to occupy a much more important place in the lay conception of religion than their position in theology warranted. They became a vivid concept, much more vivid than the virtues or any other list of sins. Literature and Art, supplied with themes by this interest in the Sins, in turn contributed to it, keeping it alive by furnishing more and more treatments of this absorbing concept.

The way in which *The Nun's Priest's Tale* relates to this is clear.

(iv) THE NUN'S PRIEST'S INTEREST IN CONTEMPORARY PHILOSOPHY AND THEOLOGY

In addition to exploiting effectively some of the more commonplace preaching techniques of his day – the animal exemplum, differing levels of textual interpretation and the Seven Deadly Sins – the Nun's Priest also shows an awareness of more recondite and immediately contemporary philosophical problems. He is particularly concerned with issues of determinism and free will: the related problems of whether God actually causes each event that happens, thereby making man merely his puppet; whether man has some element of responsible choice in what he does, and, if this is so, to what degree; and, finally, the extent to which man may have valid intimations of what is going to happen in the future. These issues, as has been suggested, were widely discussed in Chaucer's England, and, once again, we need to gain some understanding of them both to suggest the breadth of the Nun's Priest's knowledge and the particular intellectual qualities he shows in handling them.

While bearing in mind the degree of over-simplification that is inevitable in broad generalization, we may suggest that the Oxford philosophers of the fourteenth century – in particular Ockham and his disciples – had undermined much of the rational support for Christian doctrines and so opened up a seemingly unbridgeable gap between God – who could now only be known through faith and the teaching of authority – and the world. This led on the one hand to a renewed interest in the world and in natural science as a proper province for the analytical mind – one might, in this context, think of Chaucer's own interest in such matters as astronomy, an interest also shared by Chauntecleer – and, on the other hand, to an emphasis on the infinite power and apparently inscrutable will of God. As a result of this latter, there was a renewed concern with the ways in which God controlled men's lives. Remote and seemingly unknowable as he might appear, did he choose man's fate and predestine his soul – in apparent disregard for man's moral and spiritual efforts – to eternal salvation, or hell-fire, or might man's own struggles avail him?

For Ockham and his followers – such writers as Robert Holcot, for example – the most fundamental truths about the nature of God were, as we have seen, held to be logically undemonstrable. However, while the absolute freedom of God to act as he chose was recognized, it was also recognized that in the Old and New Testaments God had entered into a covenant with man by which salvation was more or less assured to those who fulfilled their side of the divine bargain. Man's moral efforts might indeed be supposed to have some efficacy in his salvation; and it was to this area – the area of agreement or covenant between God and man – that theological speculation could now be reasonably applied. As a result of positing a logically unknowable God who had, nonetheless, covenanted a relationship with man in which it might be reasonably assumed that there were clear and, to a certain extent, reciprocal obligations, the emphasis of theological speculation shifted to those parts of the covenant that concerned man and his responsibilities. Questions were asked about what man was required to do to conform to his side of the bargain and so help himself towards the promise of a likely salvation. In the words of Janet Coleman, 'Man was given ... personal responsibility as an appointed representative of God, responsible for his own life, society and the world, within the limit of the ... covenant that was stipulated by God.'

Our most useful way of expanding on these concepts will be to turn to the writing of Robert Holcot. Among the issues that Holcot discussed were these: how was man to know that he was fulfilling his side of the covenant, and, to use the titles of some of Holcot's essays: 'Is everything subjected to divine ordination?' 'Can man, assisted by grace, earn eternal life by his own merit?' 'Are we permitted to observe signs in order to know future events?' If we turn to both the lengthy discussion of dreams in *The Nun's Priest's Tale* and to that subtle, complex passage on the rights and wrongs of predestination in ll. 414–35, then we shall see that these issues are of immediate relevance to the poem.

Holcot believed that 'to those who did their very best naturally in this life God would not withhold grace'. In other words, by right action man would merit the gift of God's love that would ensure him salvation. There was, however, no absolute obligation on God's part – only a conjectured likelihood. One obvious question that now had to be asked was how was man to know that he was acting rightly? What guided him? The answer given by both Holcot and Ockham is reason. According to Ockham, reason is a sufficient guide and means of preparing the soul for grace, and Ockham defined reason as both practical knowledge gained through experience and an objective guiding principle allowing man to make correct moral choices with which to direct his will. Thus the terms of God's covenant could be understood through man's reason and man himself would receive God's help when his own reason, guiding his will, caused him to act correctly. Natural reason could show man what is right or wrong, and the freely operating will, when it does what is correct, makes a rational choice which places man in the position where he might well merit grace and salvation. Holcot repeats much of this. He too saw reason as the guiding principle of willed action and hence essential to the living of a truly moral life. Man's natural reason is, he says, a sufficient guide which allows him to understand the works of God's providence, and, while man can be far from certain that he is indeed guaranteed salvation, rational, informed and willed moral choice becomes a reliable and dignified basis for faith. To translate Holcot himself, 'man may acquire through natural reason all that is necessary to salvation'.

The bias of such a theology had at least three repercussions of importance to *The Nun's Priest's Tale*. First, it placed a considerable emphasis on the efficacious functioning of reason as a guide to the will. As such, it tended to suggest that man is in a large degree able to reason and will his way towards salvation and so, as a corollary, it tended to diminish an awareness of his fallen and sinful nature.

We should discuss here something of the ways in which these considerations relate to *The Nun's Priest's Tale*. We have already noted that in the Parson's traditional theology, error corrupts men stained with original sin by first tempting them to fleshly delights and then inclining their reason and will to believe that these are the true good. We may therefore see the intellectual but abundantly fleshly Chauntecleer, as he places love of wife before intellectual concerns and so clouds his mind, falling into errors of reason and will that certainly do not lead to his salvation. In other words, it is all very well to adopt a theology which tends to suggest that reason is a sufficient guide by which the will may make its decisions, but the idea nonetheless remains – and it is an idea deeply rooted in traditional Christian thought – that it is through just this capacity to reason that Satan tempted man and so led him to will the eating of the apple, the very act that led to his fall. Thus, while Chauntecleer to a large degree represents a fourteenth-century intellectual who is proud of his ability to reason – a capacity which it could be held was sufficient to guide the will towards correct choices of action which could lead to salvation – so also Chauntecleer's very delight in that reason, when corrupted by fleshly temptation, leads him eventually to fall into the jaws of the fox. A fourteenth-century intellectual he may be; he is also a 'type' of Adam and man's sinful and faulted reason.

A further factor that should be borne in mind is the marked extent to which these recondite theological issues – all of which could suggest man's self-sufficiency in the divine scheme of things, or, at the least, the large measure of responsibility he might be said to have for his own salvation – spread downwards from university circles to be discussed by informed laymen. Indeed, Ockham himself declared that university lecturers were pestered by old women who wondered how the will could be free if God – as he must do – has knowledge of all man's actions past, present and to come. If God does in fact know all things and is all-powerful, how can man really be said to be the master of his own fate? It is to this issue that we should now turn.

The Nun's Priest is perfectly well aware that this matter was both complex and fraught. There is, he says, 'gret altercacioun' about it and he then briefly cites three authorities on the matter: St Augustine, Boethius and the contemporary 'bishop Bradwardine'.

We have characterized the tendencies in the thought of Ockham and his disciple Holcot – somewhat too simply perhaps – as suggesting an exalted view of man's rational faculties in terms of traditional theology, tendencies which at their most extreme might have suggested that man could reason and will his way to grace and salvation. Such ideas might thus have been construed to place an undue emphasis on man's abilities at the expense of God's freedom. This problem had also been faced by St Augustine when – writing to oppose the views of Pelagius, who had similarly claimed that rational man could become the architect of his own salvation – he exposed the errors of what came to be known as the Pelagian Heresy. Archbishop Bradwardine, writing in England in the fourteenth century, believed he found himself confronting a similar position and set out to counter it in both a long Latin work significantly entitled *De causa dei contra Pelagium,* and also in a sermon preached in English to the victorious army of Edward III after the Battle of Crécy, a work which, in its turn, was translated into Latin and preserved. Bradwardine, like St Augustine before him, tended to a determinist view of man. For example, the English victory over the French, he declared, was gained neither by man's prowess and intellect, nor by the influence of the stars, but by God's decision. It was God who provided the prudent counsel that ensured victory, not the king. Similarly, the victory was not a matter of mere Fortune – or luck – since all deeds are ordained and proceed from divine providence. God, all-knowing and all-powerful, does indeed control the world in Bradwardine's view.

The third authority that the Nun's Priest cites along with Augustine and Bradwardine is Chaucer's favourite Boethius, and, in particular, the work of Boethius that Chaucer himself translated: *The Consolation of Philosophy.* In ll. 423–30, the Nun's Priest states three positions on the subject of predestination, all of which are derived from Boethius: first, what he calls 'simple necessitee', which is the through-going determinism which states that God directly ordains all things; secondly, he mentions the possibility that God knows what man will do but leaves him free to do it or not; thirdly, 'necessitee condicionel' is mentioned in which there is an element of free choice as far as the performer of the deed is concerned. And at this point – when it is evident that we have entered the thickets of metaphysical speculation – the Nun's Priest strongly affirms his reluctance to deal with such matters. Indeed, having shown that he is thoroughly familiar with modern philosophy and its difficult jargon, he states bluntly:

> I wol not han to do of swich matere.

Our expectations of a deep philosophical discourse are suddenly thwarted. This is an extraordinary dramatic coup and one which, as we shall see, points to the wry wisdom that underlines the whole Tale. Before we can go on to discuss the implications of this, however, we should summarize those expectations that Chaucer's presentation of the Nun's Priest have already aroused.

*

We have characterized the Nun's Priest as a creation of Chaucer's art and suggested that through him Chaucer is attempting to show a particular attitude towards some of the central poetic, theological and philosophical issues of his day. We have intimated that this view is a benevolently comic one and consists in part at least of a raising of intellectual and literary expectations which are humorously thwarted even in the act of being raised. For example, he alerts our philosphical interests only to deny them fulfilment. However, for this frustration of literary expectations to be successful – and, above all, comic – we should be clear from the start what such expectations are. In the case *The Nun's Priest's Tale*, we have said that the expectations revolve around a number of issues which an exemplary sermon in the form of a beast fable might be assumed to have raised in a medieval audience's mind.

Let us look first at the figure of the Nun's Priest himself, the narrator of the beast fable. We have described his initial presentation as a carefully contrived contrast to the Monk. Where the Monk is both worldly and a pompous bore, a man whose moral teaching fails to convince his audience, the Nun's Priest is, at least in his initial presentation, poor, somewhat anonymous, a man of quiet, engaging but shrewd humour who is admired by Chaucer as both a fine individual and a worthy member of his vocation. The Nun's Priest is also a literate man, well versed in both popular and more recondite matters of the faith, and fully able to deliver a sermon. Indeed, he apparently fulfils many of the requirements conventionally expected of preachers. He is modest, scholarly and lovable, dexterous in his handling of his material and able to tell a story that suggests both a surface and a deeper significance. To practise these latter skills in particular, he needs the knowledge that he shows of traditional beast fable, theology, philosophy and animal iconography, a familiarity with the different layers of textual interpretation practised by the middle ages, and an awareness of the tradition of the Seven Deadly Sins both in themselves and in their relation to traditions of animal symbolism.

It is thus possible to see the Nun's Priest operating within a framework that would have been familiar to his contemporaries. What this idea does not suggest, however – and it helps to account for the comic genius of the poem – is that while the Nun's Priest is capable of bringing to his beast fable a wide range of related moral and theological material, he does so in a way that never becomes simply didactic. He is not a tedious moralist. Rather, with an artifice that suggests a wise and very subtle mind, he constantly thwarts conventional literary expectation and exploits ambiguity for comic effect. To appreciate something of the variety of this we should look now at his presentation of his characters. We will begin with his comic hero.

4. Chauntecleer

One aspect of the presentation of Chauntecleer we should constantly bear in mind is the sheer delight his creator takes in his physical presence. For all the wealth of allusion that gathers about him, the immediate strokes by which Chauntecleer is characterized ensure that he remains a most vivid presence. Just as the marginal illustrations in the great religious manuscripts offset the splendours of the text, so Chauntecleer, with his black bill and azure legs, his delight in 'thise blisful briddes how they singe', his sexual energies, his verbal powers, and even his quick glance at the butterfly, remains the very compelling figure through whom the comic aspects of the poem are partly revealed. Likewise, the Widow's sooty 'bour and eek her halle', the dry-ditched yard with its palisade of sticks and the restricting perch on which Chauntecleer is obliged to roost, help provide him with a precise habitation. Though, like all the characters in the poem, Chauntecleer does indeed represent abstract ideas – and represents them in a way that is subtle, changing and often ironic – Chauntecleer himself never becomes a mere abstraction. He is a very engaging creation in a very real world.

In what follows, much of our discussion will inevitably focus on the structure of ideas that underlies the presentation of Chauntecleer. As a consequence, we shall perhaps run the risk of being over-serious about what is often seen as comic. The underlying and serious ideas of the poem need to be known, however, for only when we have some knowledge of them shall we be able to appreciate both the rhetorical sleight of hand by which they are presented and see how the physical and linguistic worlds of Chauntecleer are a vital contribution to the poem's comic effect. With this caveat in mind, we may proceed to discuss the following: Chauntecleer's physical setting, beauty and natural skills, his debate with his wife on the nature of dreams, his concupiscence and pride, his fall and his eventual escape from the fox. As we examine these matters, so we shall move constantly between the 'historical' or 'literal' world of the poem, stress the allegorical structure by which Chauntecleer becomes an image of man, and see man himself in relation to the eternal issues posed by the fall of Adam and the Seven Deadly Sins. We can then go on to see how these ideas are tested against a warmly human and comic wisdom.

Chauntecleer's physical setting, natural skills and beauty

Chauntecleer's beauty is placed in the most workaday of worlds. This at once makes it slightly ridiculous. The poem opens with a picture of the

Widow's cottage and her poor but virtuous life. These are beautifully described. Indeed, the opening paragraph is one of the most charming passages in all medieval English literature. We shall see later that a wealth of allusion gathers round it, but we may stress here its physical aspects, its exemplary picture of peaceful poverty and suggestion of an immemorial peasant life in which a brood of hens provides a happy old soul with the occasional luxury of an egg or two. So much, we may say, for the economics of everyday life. We may not approve of what looks like a deprived existence, but we shall miss the point entirely if we fail to appreciate the healthy content of the spry Widow and contrast this to the dangerous but comic pride of Chauntecleer. Not for him – as he thinks – is a life of quiet servitude. He is blessed with intellect, with beauty and a harem. Furthermore, he has the most remarkable voice. Indeed, he is the *nonpareil* of cockerels. And, of course, we already smile at his pretensions and take a delight in the ease with which the narrator establishes his physical presence while at the same time making us realize that Chauntecleer is an allegory of man.

The comedy here lies partly in the quick accumulation of superlatives; the peerless voice, the great natural ability, the physical beauty, the abundant opportunities for sexual release. All of this, once it has been stated, is then beautifully offset by the deadpan:

> For thilke tyme, as I have understonde,
> Bestes and briddes coude speke and singe.

We are in storyland. But the comic exaggeration already suggests an overweaning pride, a state of life too delightful to last. Further, it suggests some of the other main themes in the poem. The wonderful voice, for example, more reliable than 'an abbey orlogge', is the flourish that offsets a great natural ability to tell the time by reading the stars. In an age of digital watches with their tiresome alarms, Chauntecleer's timekeeping may seem no great matter. But we should remember that the people of the middle ages were in an altogether different and more precarious position. In large monastic institutions, for example, a degree of accurate timekeeping was absolutely essential. Though the hours of services varied with the seasons, the early morning sequence was so rapid that miscalculations could cause severe confusion. For a long while, men had only the stars to rely on, and in this passage from an eleventh-century monastic timetable, we can see how responsible the night-watchman's star-gazing needed to be:

On Christmas Day, when you see the Twins lying, as it were, on the dormitory and Orion over the chapel of All Saints, prepare to ring the bell. And on Jan. 1st, when the bright star in the Knee of Artophilax [i.e. Arcturus in Boötes] is level with the space between the first and the second window of the dormitory and lying as it were on the summit of the roof, then go and light the lamps.

It is an interesting reflection that even the most mundane of jobs required such an effort, and it is partly in this context that we should appreciate Chauntecleer's skill and the wealth of astronomical calculation that the poem provides. Clocks certainly existed by Chaucer's time, but they were far less accurate than Chauntecleer, who

> Caste up his eyen to the brighte sonne,
> That in the signe of Taurus hadde y-ronne
> Twenty degrees and oon, and somwhat more;
> And knew by kynde, and by noon other lore,
> That it was pryme, and crew with blisful stevene.

Nonetheless, we should note how on each occasion that Chauntecleer's timekeeping abilities are mentioned it is his natural facility that is emphasized. What does this mean? We may infer from it that Chauntecleer's – and therefore man's – reading the stars to tell the time is a proper use of the intellect. Timekeeping is a useful skill, a legitimate reason for interpreting the movement of the planets, and not in itself a species of dangerous intellectual pride. The forms of this will be analysed later.

Chauntecleer's beauty is also stressed from the start. His physical presence is as sumptuous and formal as a device from a knightly shield. His comb is 'redder than the fyn coral' and crenellated like a castle wall. His bill is jet. His legs are 'asur', his toes white as lilies, and his overall colour is burnished gold. This is a heraldic glory, a noble pomp, and is delightfully incongruous in the setting of a peasant's cottage. Nonetheless, Chauntecleer thinks he is the monarch of all he surveys. A scruffy yard is his empire, his world. As with man, it is all he can imagine ruling. But is there so very much to be proud of? Of course not. While men and cockerels pick their way across the earth, it may very well seem an abundant wealth. In the eyes of eternity it is nothing of the sort. The soul of the dead Troilus, for example – that so very human lover of the world's vanity – finally sees the earth in a far truer perspective:

> And doun from thennes faste he gan avyse
> This litel spot of erthe, that with the see
> Embraced is, and fully gan despyse
> This wrecched world, and held al vanitee
> To respect of the pleyn felicitee
> That is in hevene above ...

> *thennes*: there, i.e. the erratic seventh sphere of heaven
> *pleyn felicitee*: unadulterated delight

This is an abiding medieval attitude, present when not even directly stated; but such a wholehearted contempt for the world is less to the purpose here than the good-humoured satire which it prompts of Chauntecleer's worldly pride, the pride of this little Solomon in all his glory:

> Royal he was, he was namore aferd;
> He fethered Pertelote twenty tyme,
> And trad as ofte, er that it was pryme.
> He loketh as it were a grim leoun;
> And on his toos he rometh up and doun,
> Him deyned not to sette his foot to grounde.
> He chukketh, whan he hath a corn y-founde,
> And to him rennen thanne his wyves alle.
> Thus royal, as a prince is in his halle,
> Leve I this Chauntecleer in his pasture ...

It thus is clear already that the presentation of Chauntecleer and his physical world contains strong symbolic and moral elements and that these are treated in a comic way. The cockerel is a representative of man – absurd yet engaging in his worldly pride – who picks his imperious way across 'this litel spot of erthe'. Nonetheless, this snapper-up of unconsidered grains of corn is, for all his finery, merely a cockerel, albeit an abundantly – even gloriously – libidinous one. To this we should now turn.

Chauntecleer as a 'married man'

Chauntecleer's randiness is important. That cocks have a strong sexual appetite is a matter of common observation enshrined in sexual slang. There is no reason to be coy about this; indeed, we shall miss much of the point if we are. Rather, we should consider this medieval lyric with its delightfully sustained *double entendre* and wholesome bawdy. It throws much light on how some aspects of Chauntecleer would have been perceived:

> I have a gentle cock,
> Croweth me day:
> He doth me risen erly
> My matins for to say.

> I have a gentle cock,
> Comen he is of gret:
> His comb is of red coral,
> His tail is of jet.

> I have a gentle cock,
> Comen he is of kinde:
> His comb is of red coral,
> His tail is of inde.
>
> His legges ben of asor,
> So gentle and so smale;
> His spores arn of silver whit
> Into the wortewale.
>
> His eynen arn of cristal,
> Loken all in aumber:
> And every night he percheth him
> In mine lady's chaumber.

gentle: well bred   *He doth me risen erly*: he gets me up early
Comen he is of gret: descended from a distinguished line
kinde: good birth   *inde*: indigo   *asor*: azure
Into the wortewale: up to the root (of his spurs)   *Loken*: set

This is analogous to Chauntecleer 'feathering' Pertelote 'twenty tyme' and 'treading' her 'as oft'. His sensual drive is gloriously abundant, a comic overstatement of the wishes of many men. There is nothing drearily promiscuous about it. It is a positive exuberance, life enhancing and even humane. Chauntecleer can address his wife with a measure of poetry. There is real love here and, with it, its attendant complications. For example, we are encouraged to see Pertelote – initially at any rate – as a lovely courtly lady: 'curteys', 'discreet', 'debonaire' and 'compaignable'. If the description of Chauntecleer prompts us to view him as an intelligent nobleman, glorious in his finery, then Pertelote at first appears as a perfect lady from romance. But she has got Chauntecleer where she wants him. She has his heart 'loken in every lith'. This king of the backyard is apparently servant to a lady who is clearly no fool. The result of such a shrewdly observed situation is – rather charmingly – wedded bliss and love songs. The man loves his wife and still sometimes talks to her as a fashionable lover should. The wife appears content – domestic relations and her social status are, it seems, satisfactorily in her control – and, as a result, the couple sing together in perfect harmony.

But great literature rarely consists of simple delights, and the presentation of Chauntecleer the married man is far more subtle than we have so far suggested. There is, for example, a bluntly physical difficulty in the marriage: the comic problem of the night-time arrangements on the narrow perch, and the fact that the reality of Pertelote's situation is that she has to submit to the inordinate physical demands of her husband.

We have characterized Chauntecleer so far as able, libidinous, proud, courtly and married. We have seen that both partners in this marriage derive particular comforts and dissatisfactions from the arrangement and this suggests a subtle appreciation of wedlock on the part of the narrator. So completely do we identify the birds as husband and wife, however, that when some of Chauntecleer's love-talk reminds us that they are really only a cockerel and a hen, the effect is richly comic. Put simply, Pertelote is beautiful as a hen but far from an ideal of human womanhood. When Chauntecleer is at his most tender we also see that, while, as a cockerel, he may have found his ideal mate, as a representative of man – a human lover – the beauty he perceives in his wife is very much in his beholder's eye:

> whan I see the beautee of your face,
> Ye ben so scarlet-reed about your yën,
> It maketh al my drede for to dyen ...

It is this sort of tender ambiguity that makes *The Nun's Priest's Tale* so rich and so wise; and yet, once again, we need to have a knowledge of certain medieval preconceptions if we are to achieve a real understanding of the poem. We should look, for example, at what we might call the 'hard-line' theological approach to the place of such sexuality as Chauntecleer's within marriage.

Of the three legitimate states of the sexual life – virginity, widowhood and marriage – marriage was reckoned to be least worthy and the most troublesome. St Paul had admitted – somewhat grudgingly – that it is better to marry than to burn, but 'hard-line' Catholic theology refused to be locked out even by the bedroom door. We may turn to Chaucer's Parson for his advice. He defines marriage thus:

Now shaltow understonde, that matrimoine is leefful assemblinge of man and of womman, that receyven by vertu of the sacrement the bond, thurgh which they may nat be departed in al hir lyf, that is to seyn, whyl that they liven bothe. This, as seith the book, is a ful greet sacrement. God maked it, as I have seyd, in paradys, and wolde him-self be born in mariage. And for to halwen mariage, he was at a weddinge, where-as he turned water in-to wyn; which was the firste miracle that he wroghte in erthe biforn hise disciples. Trewe effect of mariage clenseth fornicacioun and replenisseth holy chirche of good linage; for that is the ende of mariage; and it chaungeth deedly sinne in-to venial sinne bitwixe hem that been y-wedded, and maketh the hertes al oon of hem that been y-wedded, as wel as the bodies.

leefful: lawful   *the book*: the Bible   *halwen*: bless
good linage: legitimate offspring

57

Marriage, in other words, is a means of avoiding promiscuity and of producing souls for the church to save. It ensures that sexuality is only a venial – as opposed to a deadly – sin. It is a state blessed by God and 'ordeyned' as monogamous. Its emotional advantage is that it 'maketh the hertes al oon of hem that been y-wedded'. However, while marriage so conceived may act as a safeguard from mortal error, it remains a state fraught with danger. All fleshly impulses tend to the 'norissinge of sinne and occasion of sin'. This is true even in the marriage bed. It was considered a Deadly Sin 'whan a man loveth any creature more than Iesu Crist oure creatour' – and this 'creature' may well be a man's wife. To be sure, the sacrament of marriage reduced the sinful status of Lust from deadly to venial, but sin it nonetheless remained 'whan a man useth his wyf, withouten sovereyn desyr of engendrure, to the honour of god, or for the entente to yelde to his wyf the dette of his body'. Chauntecleer, of course, has none of these interests in mind when he 'feathers' Pertelote. Children, God or even the welfare of his spouse are not uppermost in his mind at all. He enjoys sex for its own sake. As the Nun's Priest declares, he has performed 'more for delyt, than world to multiplye'. In the Parson's vivid image, he has been grasped by the five fingers of Lust which:

gripeth him by the reynes, for to throwen him in-to the fourneys of helle; ther-as they shul han the fyr and the wormes that evere shul lasten, and wepinge and wailinge, sharp hunger and thurst, and grimnesse of develes that shullen al to-trede hem, with-outen respit and with-outen ende.

reynes: kidneys (seat of lust)   *to-trede*: trample underfoot

As the Parson shows, Chauntecleer has passed from 'fol lookinge' to 'vileyns touchinge' and on through 'foule wordes', his declaration of his feelings, to kissing – the lover's mouth was, of course, considered the mouth of hell – to end up at 'the stinkinge dede of Lecherie' itself. According to 'hard-line' theology, Chauntecleer has made an idol of his wife and indulged his sexual appetite for its own sake. Far from honouring the sacrament of marriage, he might well have been regarded – incredible as this may seem – as having committed adultery with his own wife. In the words of the Parson once again:

The thridde spece of avoutrie is som-tyme bitwixe a man and his wyf; and that is whan they take no reward in hir assemblinge, but only to hire fleshly delyt, as seith seint Ierome; and ne rekken of no-thing but that they been assembled; by-cause that they been maried, al is good y-nough, as thinketh to hem. But in swich folk hath the devel power, as seyde the aungel Raphael to Thobie; for in hir assemblinge they putten Iesu Crist out of hir herte, and yeven hem-self to alle ordure.

avoutrie: adultery   *take no reward etc.*: have no intentions during copulation except physical pleasure   *assemblinge*: copulation
by-cause: since   *ordure*: filthiness

This conception of marriage suggests that, in addition to the subtle but movingly realistic personal situation Chauntecleer finds himself in, he has also placed his soul in peril. Far from seeing marriage as a relationship in which a man 'sholde loven his wyf by discrecioun, paciently and atemprely; and thanne is she as though it were his suster', Chauntecleer views it as a licensed indulgence.

And surely we sympathize with him. The comic excesses of his potency are life-enhancing, invigorating. The 'hard-line' view is repellent by contrast. We want to reject it. This ambiguity, this confrontation of seemingly irreconcilable views, lies at the heart of the Nun's Priest's view of love, and we shall return to it often. We may note here – as a foretaste of our discussion of his able, kindly and quick-witted presentation of his story – that while the Nun's Priest is clearly familiar with conventional teaching on marriage, he also has his own more humane and generous appreciation of the married state. The way he deals with such conflicts accounts not only for the humour of the poem but, as we shall see, for its technical sophistication and, most importantly, its comic wisdom, its realization of the complexities of human life, and hence its timeless warmth.

For the moment, however, we need to develop rather more fully our view of the 'hard-line' theology that lends its significance to the presentation of Chauntecleer. So far we have seen how Lust is a danger even in marriage. We have seen it as one of the ways in which sin can 'put a man in greet thraldom', divert his mind and body from their proper responsibilities towards the soul and so threaten him with divine punishment. Through his Lust, Chauntecleer has made his mind a servant to the senses. We should now widen the context of our discussion of this by turning to the long, noisy passage on dreams in the Tale and see how the conclusions of this very learned debate are suddenly forgotten in an excess of uxorious desire. We should see, in other words, how Chauntecleer's love of his wife – his uxoriousness – leads him to forget what his reason interprets as a dream-warning from God and so starts the process by which he falls into the mouth of the fox. As we do so, so we should be aware that the pattern of his folly imitates the process by which Adam, beguiled by his wife, forgot the commandments of God and so also fell into sin. As Chauntecleer repeats this primal error, so he is both a 'type' of Adam and an image of all mankind. It is through this that the discussion of marriage merges with the discussions of philosophy and theology.

'Maistrie' and the debate on the nature of dreams

In our initial description of the marriage between Chauntecleer and Pertelote we suggested that the cockerel saw his wife in at least two aspects: as a courtly lady and as an object for his sexual release. As far as he is concerned, there is both idealism and self-indulgence in his marriage. We characterized Pertelote as both the recipient of Chauntecleer's excessive demands and as a shrewd but loving woman well aware that she has the heart of Chauntecleer 'loken in every lith'. Thus, in some ways at least, Pertelote has the upper hand. It is this aspect of Chauntecleer's marriage we should examine first to prepare us for the debate on dreams. In other words, we must consider Chauntecleer as a henpecked husband, a man whose wife appears to have the 'maistrie' or dominant role in the marriage.

The discussion of who should be the dominant partner in a marriage clearly interested Chaucer considerably. *The Franklin's Tale* – that most exquisite discussion of gentility – is deeply concerned with it. The Wife of Bath is also fascinated by the subject and debates it at great length and with a deal of misinformation, only to tell a tale which starts with rape – the most extreme form of male dominance – and ends up with the lady appearing to have the upper hand while actually submitting to her husband. Our business here is 'hard-line' theology, however, and we may turn to the Parson once again to learn what was the acceptable state of things. What did the church think about 'maistrie'?

The Parson's view is clear: 'ther-as the womman hath the maistrie, she maketh to muche desray; ther neden none ensamples of this. The experience of day by day oghte suffyse.' In other words, men should always be the dominant partner. This view is based – naturally enough – on an analogy between the relation of every man and wife to the relation of Adam and Eve. In orthodox theology, God created Eve from Adam's rib – thereby signifying companionship – and not from his head, which would have suggested 'lordshipe'. While the man should be patient, respectful and loyal to his wife – even dying for her if necessary – the requirements made of the woman were obedience, service, modesty in dressing and discretion, while, 'aboven alle worldly thing she sholde loven hir housbonde with al hir herte, and to him be trewe of her body'. There is no doubt about Pertelote's fidelity – though Chauntecleer has his paramours – but many of the other reticent qualities described here are lacking. Pertelote is forceful, down-to-earth and clearly wishes to guide her husband in intellectual matters. To help in this, she enjoys a robust vocabulary and a vigorous tongue.

This is clear right from her first 'fy for shame!' which is uttered before she has even discovered what ails her groaning husband. When he has described his dream to her she again rounds on him in a long speech (ll. 88–149) that begins with superbly knockabout shrewishness and then develops the idea that dreams are fantasies springing from an upset constitution. Pertelote is very proud of her housewifely common sense here, her little learning and her verbal skills. There is not a strain of fantasy about what she says. Pertelote's is a world of emetics and pulling yourself together. It is the husband who is the superstitious one. Pertelote reveals herself like one of those who think today that life's chronic uncertainties can be pushed aside with aerobics and a high-fibre diet. By so strongly affirming this point of view she attempts to assert her 'maistrie'.

In fact, the whole issue of dreaming was very complex, and, just as Pertelote is a medieval example of an abiding type, so Chauntecleer appears by contrast as one of those who think that dreams are the royal road to understanding deep-seated, even cosmic powers. The two attitudes could hardly be more contrary. Both have something in their favour, however, and both run rapidly to extremes. Through them the Tale is provided with many things: contrast both intellectual and comic, and the opportunity to air an important issue in a way which amusingly illustrates the issue of 'maistrie' in marriage. Further, as we have mentioned, the full context of the discussion relates man and wife, their conflicts and passions, to the timeless actions of Adam and Eve and the fall of man.

Virtually the whole of the debate on dreams is taken from material in Robert Holcot's *Super sapientiam Salomonis*, a commentary on the Book of Wisdom. We have already suggested Holcot's place in the intellectual life of Chaucer's period. We are dealing here with a popularizer who, particularly through the work just mentioned, became suddenly famous, a man whose work was read for the next two centuries. One of Holcot's main interests was to help define the areas that might guide men's reason towards an understanding of the rules governing the covenant between himself and God. As we have seen, the proper following of these rules would, it was hoped, almost certainly lead to salvation. The Wisdom literature of the Bible was thus a particular interest and, in the words of Beryl Smalley, 'appealed to Holcot and his contemporaries as the biblical equivalent of the didactic literature on political and moral science ... which they loved so well'. She also notes that on some manuscript copies of Holcot's commentary on the Book of Wisdom appears an inscription which has an obvious relevance to the princely Chauntecleer: '"Although wisdom is found in each part of Holy Scripture it is contained especially and in a particular form in this book, where kings and princes are instructed on the worship of God and on right conduct."' This helps to suggest that *The Nun's Priest's Tale*'s employment of Holcot places the poem in the mainstream of contemporary medieval speculation.

Just as we should never forget the vivid physical presence of Chauntecleer and Pertelote, so we should always remember the vigour with which they argue with each other. The argument is opened by Pertelote, and her hard-hitting speech achieves a wealth of comic effect. Gone at once is the queen of romance, the 'discreet and debonaire' lady of the introduction. Pertelote the queen now becomes Pertelote the shrill-tongued housewife whose pillow talk is marvellously at odds with her supposed social role. It is also at odds with the proper meekness required of her wifely status in 'hard-line' theology. Pertelote wants 'maistrie' and she reckons to get it by telling her husband that he is no man. 'Have you no mannes herte, and han a berd?' she asks. Such dreams as Chauntecleer's are the result of an upset stomach, she declares. They are fantasies that wise men should ignore. A good emetic is what Chauntecleer needs, and Pertelote clearly takes enormous pride – a notable point – in the herbal wisdom that she then provides us with. We do not usually associate queens with laxatives, but the resulting comedy is excellent.

Much of Pertelote's theory of dreams derives, as we have said, from Holcot. Two lectures in the *Super sapientiam Salomonis* discuss dreams, and, according to Holcot, three types of men are particularly likely to have dreams which mean something: lovers, the melancholy and the insane. Such significative dreams derive in their turn from five sources: some derive from an excess of a particular humour in a man's body, and this we shall discuss in more detail in a moment; others derive from the mind when it is worried about a friend or enemy; some are prompted by good spirits, others by evil; finally some dreams derive directly from the influence of the heavenly bodies as they are moved by the will of God. In other words, they are derived from the stars and are an expression of God's purposes. According to Holcot's curious remark, this latter type of dream is more likely to affect birds than reasonable and prudent men. But should we really give any credence at all to such dreams? Holcot states – in Latin – that 'some dreams are worthy of being believed'. Divination through dreams *is* permissible on occasions – Holcot has just been discussing the dreams that forewarned the destruction of the firstborn of Egypt but divination cannot be applied to all dreams, and is, anyway, a very hazardous proceeding. This is at least in part a bow to conventional theology. According to the Parson: 'divgnailes [divinations] as by ... dremes ... is deffended [forbidden] by god and by al holy chirche. For which they been acursed, til they come to amendement, that on swich filthe setten hir bileve.' Holcot certainly states in both lectures the commonplace: 'do not trouble yourself about dreams, for dreams deceive many', and this idea is clearly reflected in Pertelote's 'do no fors of dremes'. The phrase derives from the *Disticha* of 'Catoun'.

Indeed, as far as Pertelote is concerned, dreams are just a 'vanitee' deriving from an upset in the humours, particularly choler and melancholy. A superfluity of 'rede colera' is responsible, in Pertelote's view, for many of the things Chauntecleer has dreamt of: biting russet animals and 'contek' – in other words, just the hazards that Chauntecleer will indeed face later that morning. Melancholy, on the other hand, leads to dreams of 'blake develes' – in other words, a 'col-fox'. In thus dismissing dreams as illusions incapable of revealing the future, Pertelote provides many unwitting details in the portrait of Russel. By a further irony, what she proposes to Chauntecleer is not vigilance but a violent course of laxatives.

Chauntecleer will have none of them. He knows Pertelote's medicines of old:

> I seye forther-more,
> That I ne telle of laxatyves no store,
> For they ben venimous, I woot it wel;
> I hem defye, I love hem never a del.

But the suggestion that Chauntecleer be purged 'binethe, and eek above', is not all that Pertelote has achieved here. She has provided much comedy in her attempt to assert her 'maistrie' while, in her citing of 'autoritee' and her detailed description of the humours theory of dreams, she has both provided material for *The Canterbury Tales* as a compilatio and overstepped the proper bounds of feminine propriety. Chauntecleer counters with a vigorous and lengthy speech in which he elaborates the other side of the argument. He is both making a point and trying to re-establish his 'maistrie'.

Much of Chauntecleer's material is expressed through moral stories – exempla inserted into what is already an exemplary text. This suggests a number of points. First of all, the use of such a technique is here innately comic. We do not expect cockerels to have had a university education. This in turn prompts the idea that such learning is, in its context, being lightly satirized. But we should be careful. Proverbs, citations and exemplary stories were far more firmly a part of the medieval mind than they are of ours. We rather despise proverbs and tend to dismiss them as clichés. The middle ages, however, had such phrases in abundance. They helped to relate specific events to the common wisdom of experience. The same went for exemplary stories. The great historian Johan Huizinga wrote of this tendency thus:

> In the minds of the Middle Ages every event, every case, fictitious or historic, tends to crystallize, to become a parable, an example, a proof, in order to be applied as a standing instance of a general moral truth. In the same way every utterance becomes a dictum, a maxim, a text. For every question of conduct, Scripture, legend, history, literature, furnish a crown of examples or of types, together making up a sort of moral clan, to which the matter in question belongs. If it is desired to make someone pardon an offence, all the Biblical cases of pardon are enumerated to him: if to dissuade him from marrying, all the unhappy marriages of antiquity are cited.

It would thus be quite wrong to characterize Chauntecleer's speech as mere pedantry. It is wholly characteristic of its period – its material is, after all, taken from Holcot – while it is also very vivid, and, as we shall see, a crucial aspect of Chauntecleer's intellectual pride.

Chauntecleer cites a wide range of exemplary incidents and authorities from both the classics and scripture. The first two tales in particular – those concerning the murder and the shipwreck – are singularly vivid and self-contained. Both also had a long history of being cited in the way that Chauntecleer uses them here. The two stories originated in ancient Greece, were retold by Cicero, and were paraphrased by both Albertus Magnus and Valerius Maximus, Holcot himself deriving them from the latter. The first tale is particularly grim. Two friends – Chaucer makes them pilgrims – become separated. The one who finds his lodging 'in a stalle' appears twice to his friend to warn him of his imminent murder and 'atte thridde tyme' to tell him he is dead. The tale is full of violence, ghosts, torture and a corpse 'that mordred was al newe'. In telling his version, Chauntecleer intensifies the horror of the original, highlights the scepticism of the surviving friend, and breaks the suspense by revealing the outcome of the dream half-way through his retelling. To drive home his point even more firmly, Chauntecleer parodies Pertelote's 'No-thing, god wot, but vanitee, in sweven is.' A good reader – and this is an indication of how important it is to remember that *The Nun's Priest's Tale* is part of an oral tradition of poetry – will almost certainly emphasize the first and last words of Chauntecleer's:

> *Him* thoughte his dreem nas but a *vanitee*.

Such a tone heightens the emphasis on violent death in the story and allows us to hear Chauntecleer establishing his dominance over his wife.

Chauntecleer's second story concerns a man who was warned in a dream not to sail and so stayed ashore and escaped drowning. Chauntecleer's chief addition here – and it is a very effective one – is the introduction of an even more sceptical friend than we find in the first story. He too calls dreams 'vanitees' and declares that men dream of absurd things like owls or apes. Of course he is trying to belittle such matters. Perhaps he is unaware that owls could represent unclean sensuality and that apes were considered 'types' or images of the devil, the fowler who traps small birds or virtuous souls. Such imagery throws a fine ironic light on the Nun's Priest's story; but, ignorant of such lore himself, the sceptical friend decides to sail and goes to his sudden and violent death.

The remaining stories are shorter. Chauntecleer's third exemplum is taken from a saint's life: that of St Kenelm. This murder of an innocent is particularly unpleasant, and Chauntecleer's version emphasizes the naïve child's inability to avoid the death which his nurse has warned him against. St Kenelm is yet another victim of an unregarded dream. After this – and Chauntecleer's statement that he had 'lever than my sherte' that Pertelote had read this story – he cites Macrobius, a very popular authority on dreams whom Chaucer had known almost from the start of his career. Chauntecleer then moves on to the biblical Daniel, Joseph and Pharaoh. He concludes with two classical stories: the death of Croesus – which the Monk also tells – and Andromache's dream of the death of Hector, which is a medieval invention.

Chauntecleer's is thus a formidable and engaging speech enlivened by vivid anecdotes and vigorous asides. A further point should also be stressed. The majority of the dreamers in the exemplary stories that he tells have a special, close relationship with God. In the case of Joseph and Pharaoh, this is obvious. Joseph's dreams divined God's truths, Pharaoh's his curses. Kenelm is a saint. Again, in the first exemplum, not only do the travellers of the original become pilgrims, but Chauntecleer interrupts the narrative with the following apostrophe to God:

> O blisful god, that art so Iust and trewe!
> Lo, how that thou biwreyest mordre alway!
> Mordre wol out, that see we day by day.
> Mordre is so wlatsom and abhominable
> To god, that is so Iust and resonable,
> That he ne wol nat suffre it heled be;
> Though it abyde a yeer, or two, or three,
> Mordre wol out, this my conclusioun.

65

In other words, there is a strongly implied suggestion here that Chauntecleer would like to see himself in a similarly favoured position. As a result, there is a distinct bias in his account of his own dream to showing that it is significative because it resulted from divine instigation. God is clearly directing his welfare. Certainly, the dream does not correspond to any of the other four sources of significant dreams analysed by Holcot. For example, Chauntecleer himself declares that it is not the result of an upset in his humours. It does not come from a mind worried about a friend or an enemy either. It is prompted neither by good nor bad spirits, and so there remains only those dreams which, in Holcot's opinion:

> are caused in a man by the virtue [i.e., the power or operative influence] of supracelestial bodies. For heavenly bodies, by causing virtue to flow into our bodies, alter our bodies in sleep, and then it happens that the imagination forms for itself appearances and images similar to the qualities caused in the body by the heavens; and thus there appear to the mind some future effects, such as concerning wars, or fertility or sterility of land and of the like, which have their cause from heavenly bodies, just as occurred with the dream of Pharaoh concerning the seven kine and the seven ears of grain; Genesis [41].

Such dreams, prompted by God's moving the planets, are indeed prophecies. Further, such dreams as Chauntecleer's, coming in the early morning, when, as Dante declared, 'our mind, more a pilgrim from the flesh and less captive to thoughts, is in its visions almost divine', were regarded as being particularly prophetic. We should also recall that Holcot himself somewhat strangely declared that birds receive the influence of heavenly bodies moved by the will of God far more readily than rational, prudent man. Finally, and to settle the matter, the Nun's Priest himself appears in no doubt that Chauntecleer's dream is indeed significative:

> O Chauntecleer, acursed be that morwe,
> That thou into that yerd flough fro the bemes!
> Thou were full well y-warned by thy dremes,
> That thilke day was perilous to thee.

But Chauntecleer takes no more notice of his dream than the major figures in his exemplary stories do of theirs. Why?

To answer this we need to draw together some of the issues we have been discussing, though we must bear in mind that at this stage our answer to the question as to why Chauntecleer refused to take any notice of his dream can only be a partial one. Much of it will be dependent on aspects of the 'hard-line' theology we have already examined. Later, when we come to see something more of the richness and ambiguity with which the Nun's Priest surrounds his presentation of Chauntecleer – when we come to appreciate his subtle rhetoric and humane, comic wisdom – then we will be able to examine Chauntecleer's turning away from his dreams in more detail. But, for the moment, we should place the responsibility for ignoring his dream warnings firmly on his sinful uxoriousness, his excessive love of his wife. He has, in his long speech, countered her arguments to his own satisfaction. By speaking with vigour and at even greater length than she, he has, he believes, re-established his 'maistrie'. He knows for certain that dreams may indeed have significance. He has, it seems, read most of the available literature on the subject. He is a well-informed and up-to-date intellectual. Like many intellectuals, however, he likes to live on the perilous edge of his ideas. Thus Chauntecleer has, he believes, been instructed in a fairly direct way by the Almighty. God is, it appears, concerned in men's – and cockerels' – welfare, prompting both in the right direction. But men and cockerels fail to take notice of him. Their reason does not always guide their will. They pay no attention to it. Instead – like Adam – they turn to their wives and to fleshly love. Chauntecleer looks on his spouse and is at once 'fondly overcome with female charm'. He has re-established his 'maistrie' only to lose it immediately in uxorious passion. In the resulting excess of his very real love for Pertelote he forgets his fears and becomes a 'type' of Adam and all sinful humanity. The couple fly down from the perch, Chauntecleer slakes his comic – but, considered in terms of 'hard-line' theology, excessive – sexual desires, and we are left with a most delightful picture of Chauntecleer reading the stars in order to fulfil his humble but useful purpose of telling the time.

Having thus repeated the sin of Adam – having descended into the mortal world of error through uxorious desire – Chauntecleer then struts through the Widow's yard and is, for all the world, like an aristocrat in his garden of love:

> 'The sonne,' he sayde, 'is clomben up on hevene
> Fourty degrees and oon, and more, y-wis.
> Madame Pertelote, my worldes blis,
> Herkneth thise blisful briddes how they singe,
> And see the fresshe floures how they springe;
> Ful is myn herte of revel and solas.'

What arrogance there is in this fallen cockerel's condescension to the 'blisful briddes' – and what sheer delight. This is the pride of the world. Here is the little monarch 'in al his pryde' accompanied by his harem, roaming up and down 'royal, as a prince is in his halle'. And, just as the 'hard-line' view of his sexual appetite conflicts with our comic delight in it, so our joy in Chauntecleer's pride offsets what the conservative

67

medieval mind would have seen as our proper contempt for the world. Chauntecleer's expression of his pride reminds us that the world is something more than a thoroughfare full of woe, however. We too delight in it. It is a delight we cannot deny.

Chauntecleer's capture and escape

Nonetheless, 'ever the latter ende of Ioye is wo'. Chauntecleer has been forewarned of the coming danger in his dreams but has set those warnings aside. In his rush of fleshly appetite he has let desire fog his reason and prompt his will. A thrall to desire, he is now also a hostage to Fortune. He is a free and rational agent no longer. And Fortune comes in the shape of the fox. At first, Chauntecleer's natural feelings tell him to run away:

> For naturelly a beest desyreth flee
> Fro his contrairie, if he may it see,
> Though he never erest had seyn it with his yë.

But the fox's flattery panders to Chauntecleer's Pride, the Deadly Sin he has been so gloriously indulging. The fox pretends he wants to hear Chauntecleer's wondrous voice. He rhapsodizes over its beauty and, as we have seen, places this in the context of the family pride of Chauntecleer's clan – a misplaced vanity that has already led to the death of Chauntecleer's parents. As with our discussion of uxorious Lust, so here, as we look at Chauntecleer's Pride, we should turn to see what the Parson has to say on this matter.

The Parson's analysis is particularly rich in insights concerning the 'hard-line' theological content of *The Nun's Priest's Tale*. He sees Pride as springing from three grounds: goods of nature, goods of fortune and goods of grace. Goods of nature include 'beautee, gentrye, franchise'. These are the qualities that go with aristocratic good breeding and are clearly evident in Chauntecleer, whose physical loveliness and noble bearing we have frequently commented on. Other gifts of nature – gifts which we might class generally as intelligence – include 'good wit, sharp understondynge ... vertu naturel, good memorie'. Chauntecleer again has these in abundance. We have seen his intelligence and ability to understand a subtle argument, his memory for these and his natural ability. Ironically, they are all made particularly evident in the discussion of dreams. The Parson's second category – the goods of fortune – are these: 'richesses, highe degrees of lordshipes, preisinges of the peple'. Again, Chauntecleer has these. He is a lord, while the 'preisinges' he receives are, of course, central to his fall. Finally we should turn to the goods of grace. Among these are the 'science' or learning which, yet again, Chauntecleer particularly relishes.

All of these possessions are things that most people want; but, as the Parson shows, 'it is a ful greet folye a man to pryden him in any of hem alle'. Physical beauty, for example, can quickly lead to a corruption of the soul through Lust. We have already seen that this certainly applies to Chauntecleer. Again, 'to pryde him of his gentrye is ful greet folye' for this makes a man – or even a cockerel – forget that all are equal in the eyes of God and the face of death. As the Parson also points out, 'Now certes, a man to pryde him in the goodes of grace is an outrageous folye; for thilke yiftes [gifts] of grace that sholde have turned him to goodnesse and to medicine, turneth him to venim and to confusion.' Finally the Parson turns to the goods of fortune. What he has to say about the perils of these could stand as an epigraph to the poem:

who-so prydeth him in the goodes of fortune, he is a ful greet fool; for som-tyme is a man a greet lord by the morwe, that is a caitif and a wrecche er it be night: and somtyme the richesse of a man is cause of his deeth; somtyme the delyces of a man is cause of the grevous maladye thurgh which he dyeth. Certes, the commendacion of the peple is sometyme ful fals and ful brotel for to triste; this day they preyse, tomorwe they blame. God woot, desyr to have commendacion of the peple hath caused deeth to many a bisy man.

caitif: one in the lowest state of fortune
delyces: pleasures   *brotel:* uncertain

Poor Chauntecleer, in terms of 'hard-line' theology, he is indeed in a parlous state. He is a personification of all aspects of Pride, even the vaingloriousness which the Parson defines as: 'to have pompe and delyt in ... temporel hynesse, and glorifie ... in this worldly estaat'.

Such Pride has its fall. Russel – whose own relation to the Seven Deadly Sins we shall discuss in a moment – flatters Chauntecleer by praising his voice. It is the oldest element in the story. Once again, prudent intelligence is overcome by delight in worldly things. The will is corrupted. Unseeing and absurd, Chauntecleer closes his eyes and stretches out his neck to sing:

> This Chauntecleer stood hye up-on his toos,
> Strecching his nekke, and heeld his eyen cloos,
> And gan to crowe loude for the nones;
> And daun Russel the fox sterte up at ones,
> And by the gargat hente Chauntecleer,
> And on his bak toward the wode him beer,
> For yet ne was ther no man that him sewed.

With what vividness and speed this image of Pride falls into peril. Narrative detail and allegorical significance are perfectly matched.

But the daring intellectual whose uxoriousness has blinded him to dreams that warned of the peril he now finds himself in, this prince whose family pride and personal vaingloriousness have got the better of his natural wariness, is not wholly without help. If Chauntecleer's philosophy and his breeding cannot assist him in his plight, his quick wits can. He has a full measure of 'cunning'. Lying on the fox's back and being swept off to his destruction – the visual aspect of this is again particularly comic and vivid – Chauntecleer can turn the tables on his foe. By a nice paradox, he appeals to Russel's own pride. He suggests that the fox turn, taunt his pursuers and boast of his skill. And, just as Chauntecleer succumbed to flattery, so does the fox:

> The fox answerde, 'in feith, it shal be don,' –
> And as he spak that word, al sodeinly
> This cok brak from his mouth deliverly,
> And heighe up-on a tree he fleigh anon.

It is not a mighty mind that leads to Chauntecleer's salvation, it is his natural quick-wittedness. The effect is wonderfully comic.

Chauntecleer and three other Sins

Chauntecleer has learned his lesson. Safe in the tree (we may perhaps think of it as a 'type' or representation of the cross), he is a wiser man – or bird. Let us examine this and relate various aspects of Chauntecleer's fall, escape and subsequent self-knowledge to further aspects of the Seven Deadly Sins. As we have mentioned, it was considered that a man who had committed one of these would naturally go on to commit several more.

We have established how – in the 'hard-line' view – Chauntecleer is a victim both of his Pride and of his uxoriousness, the excessive love of his wife which blinds his reason to the promptings of his intellect, perverts his will and so leads to his fall in a way that is directly analogous to the fall of Adam. He is thus a victim of his own special form of Lust. We have seen that he persists in a state of sin, and seen also that the Nun's Priest presents this comically – even in a life-enhancing way – rather than in drab and negative terms. However, if we set aside for the moment the complications that this twofold approach suggests and concentrate instead on the implications that the fall raises for 'hard-line' theology, then we shall see that Chauntecleer's persistence in both Pride and Lust is an example of what the Parson calls 'malice', that propensity to evil which he sees as underlying Envy and which he describes as: 'hardnesse of herte in wikkednesse, or elles the flesh of man is so blind, that he considereth nat that he is in sinne, or rekketh [cares] nat that he is in sinne; which is the hardnesse of the devel.' Thus hardened in his ways, heedless of his warning dreams, betrayed by Pride, Lust and the malice that underlies Envy, Chauntecleer is also a victim of two more of the Seven Deadly Sins: Avarice and Sloth.

Avarice is most commonly associated with hoarding money. We tend to use it as a synonym for miserliness. Certainly, in the later middle ages, when the Seven Deadly Sins were adapted to a mercantile rather than a hierarchical and feudal society, popular interpretations of Avarice – which, with some biblical authority, took the place of Pride as the chief of the Deadly Sins – came to stress this conception. We can even find strong elements of it in the Parson's presentation of vice. However, at the start of his section on Avarice he quotes St Augustine's definition of the Sin, calling Avarice 'likerousnesse [a strong desire] in herte to have erthely thinges'. He then goes on to declare that Avarice is not only directed towards the hoarding of money and income 'but somtyme in science and in glorie'. That Chauntecleer desires glory is obvious. It is precisely to achieve this that he acts so foolishly and puts himself in danger. Only when he has escaped does he realize that the fox has set out to 'bigyle' him. Chauntecleer then realizes that he has been one that 'winketh, whan he sholde see'.

The Nun's Priest adds to this by suggesting that not only has the proud Chauntecleer been deceived by flattery but that the cockerel has also been slack and careless – in other words slothful.

The Parson's term for this Deadly Sin – and his analysis is a shrewd presentation of its origins in the listlessness and melancholia that sometimes border on despair – is 'Accidie'. He is well aware of how Accidie leads from simple carelessness to the neglecting of day-to-day safety. Indeed, in this part of his definition, he comes close to the Nun's Priest's own words:

Now certes, this foule sinne Accidie is eek a ful greet enemy to the lyflode of the body; for it ne hath no purveaunce agayn temporel necessitee; for it forsleweth and forsluggeth, and destroyeth alle goodes temporeles by reccheleesnesse.

lyflode: means of living   *purveaunce*: foresight   *temporel necessitee*: worldly (mis)fortune   *forsleweth*: idly wastes   *temporeles*: worldly *reccheleesnesse*: carelessness

It is just this aspect of Accidie that the Nun's Priest drives home as the moral of his fable in lines 616–17. However, when we come to discuss the rhetorical nature of *The Nun's Priest's Tale* we shall see that these matters are nowhere as simple as they seem.

*

Our initial characterization of Chauntecleer stressed his vivid physical presence and widely ranging allegorical significance. We have shown the comic contrast between his conceit and his farmyard world, and suggested that such a contrast is one of the means by which Chauntecleer's intellectual abilities and social position are gently satirized. We have seen too that his marriage is, on a literal level, described through a shrewd combination of courtly refinement and exuberant desire. His wife has his heart 'loken in every lith', knows this and tries to use it to exploit her 'maistrie'. She is both his idealized lady and the object for his sexual release. We have seen too that, on the allegorical and tropological levels, Chauntecleer's marriage presents him not just in a touching human relationship but as a 'type' of Adam, an eternal image of man. Just as Adam's reason was clouded by love for his wife and so led his will into the errors that caused his fall, so Chauntecleer, apparently the recipient of a divine forewarning, forgets his dream in an excess of uxoriousness and, while revelling in his subsequent Pride, falls into the mouth of devilish fox. We have seen indeed that Chauntecleer may be regarded as a personification of Pride, the chief of the Seven Deadly Sins. For example, we have noted that he glories in the gifts of nature, fortune and grace, and that, once his reason, already clouded by uxorious Lust, has misled his will, so his worldly Pride – his vainglory – leads him into just the dangers his forgotten dream had warned him about. Further, his Pride also leads him into the dangers posed by other Deadly Sins, in particular the hardness of heart in sin that underlies Envy, an avaricious desire to assert his social prestige, and, above all perhaps, a slothful negligence. However, if Chauntecleer's reason is not a reliable way for him to interpret what he sees as the promptings of God revealed in his dream, he is saved on the physical level at least by his sheer comic quick-wittedness. He turns the tables on the fox, escapes, and, it appears, learns his lesson. At least he realizes how foolish he has been.

We have stressed that such an interpretation of Chauntecleer's character through the tenets of 'hard-line' theology is not to be taken as the simple message of the poem, its be all and end all. Indeed, *The Nun's Priest's Tale* is a most complex work in which the ideas of 'hard-line' theology are tested against the narrator's warm and humane love of worldly things. These aspects of the presentation of Chauntecleer are, of course, mostly dependent on the Nun's Priest's own comments and descriptive emphases, and our understanding of Chauntecleer will not be complete until we have described them. Nonetheless, since this ambiguity also applies to most of the other characters in the poem – particularly the Widow – it will be as well if we look at these figures first and then go on to describe how the Nun's Priest comments on and criticizes conventional associations. It is this that fully reveals the comic genius of the poem.

5. Pertelote, Russel and the Widow

Pertelote

Our analysis of Chauntecleer inevitably suggested something of the qualities of his wife. We saw that her portrayal was subtle, various, and held within it something of the ambiguities that characterize the poem as a whole. For example, we heard how on occasions Chauntecleer addressed Pertelote in terms befitting a courtly lady. Pertelote is queen of the hen run and has clearly established her precedence over her seven rivals. However, we have seen that she also tries to establish her 'maistrie'. If she is at first glimpsed as 'discreet and debonaire', a lady well able to be 'curteys', she is also, and by a nice paradox, a wife in a subservient position, while being dogmatic, down-to-earth and proud of her common-sense skills. Through these apparent contradictions the poem combines two medieval conventions in the literary presentation of women – the courtly lady of romance and elements of the middle-class spouse of 'fabliaux', or stories of low-life. Such contrasts suggest a range of responses in marriage. In addition, they are inherently comic and lend a vigour to the poem that keeps it rooted in a bluntly physical world: Pertelote's world of emetics and of being purged 'binethe, and eek above'. In this respect, it is a particularly shrewd contrast that makes the husband a dreamer, the believer in omens. Pertelote, as we have seen, thinks dreams are nothing more than a 'vanitee', an illusion.

The speech in which Pertelote sets out these ideas – the speech also in which she tries to assert her 'maistrie' – moves with energy from taunts about Chauntecleer's manliness, to what seems a comic and inappropriate pedantry about dreams – this in material derived from Holcot – and then on to a comprehensive list of natural laxatives and cheerful reassurance:

> Be mery, housbond, for your fader kin!
> Dredeth no dreem.

As Pertelote makes the speech, so she characterizes her hale and hearty attitude to the world, tries to establish her dominance and contributes to the debate on the nature of dreams. This latter is achieved with some subtlety, for not only does it provide a particular and valid point of view,

it also inconspicuously undermines that view by simultaneously suggesting and deriding as mere effects of indigestion some of the most obvious
physical characteristics of Russel himself. In satirizing prophetic dreams,
in believing that they have no significance, Pertelote unwittingly manages
to convey some of the most salient features of the danger Chauntecleer's
dream has warned him against – great, red and black contentious beasts.

The beginning and end of Chauntecleer's lengthy reply also throws light
on the nature of his marriage to Pertelote. If Chauntecleer can at times
address her as a great lady should be addressed, he too can lapse into
vigorous demotic speech, show Pertelote that he has read far more than
she, and then, at the close, change the subject to love talk. If Pertelote has
her husband's heart 'lokken in every lith', in the end she has to surrender
'maistrie' to him. We are then told of their love-making and see them
strutting like a princely couple across the Widow's back yard.

The presentation of Pertelote we have described so far has been various:
queen, housewife and chief spouse, a woman concerned about 'maistrie',
loquacious, down-to-earth, domineering and dominated. But Pertelote
also has her part to play in the presentation of 'hard-line' theology. If
Chauntecleer represents – or is a 'type' of – Adam, then Pertelote in a
sense stands for Eve. She is the woman who misleads her husband, whose
beauty diverts his reason from its proper function and so contributes to
his fall. But just as the 'hard-line' presentation of Chauntecleer is offset
by the apparently more humane perceptions of the narrator, so, even
more, the 'hard-line' image of Pertelote is contradicted by the Nun's Priest
himself. He can, for the purposes of consistency, toe the line. He can and
indeed does indulge in some conventional anti-feminism:

> Wommennes counseils been ful ofte colde;
> Wommannes counseil broghte us first to wo,
> And made Adam fro paradys to go,
> Ther-as he was ful mery, and wel at ese.

But this is far from all he has to say on the matter. He has his own
appreciation of women – an appreciation that Harry Bailey will joke
about when the Tale is done. And the Nun's Priest feels obliged to add
here:

> But for I noot, to whom it mighte displese,
> If I counseil of wommen wolde blame,
> Passe over, for I seyde it in my game.
> Rede auctours, wher they trete of swich matere,
> And what thay seyn of wommen ye may here.
> Thise been the cokkes wordes, and nat myne;
> I can noon harm of no womman divyne.

We shall return to this ambiguity later. It is an aspect of the rhetorical sophistication of the poem, and it is best described in that context. For the moment, we should look first at the delightful picture of this queen of the hen run enjoying her dust-bath, and then at her reactions to the abduction of Chauntecleer. These latter are particularly amusing, and again point to the rhetorical sophistication of the poem.

As Chauntecleer is being snatched away, his wife adds her voice to the cacophony that breaks out. While her lamentations are distinctly comic, we should also place them in a historical setting. This is important, for, if we contrast Pertelote's expression of her feelings to those we usually allow ourselves today, then the contrast will be far more extreme than was intended. To be sure, Pertelote's outburst is compared to that made at the fall of the Troy, to 'Hasdrubales wyf' or the spouses of the senators murdered by Nero, but we should remember that royal mourning in the middle ages – and Pertelote is Chauntecleer's queen – was conducted on a heroic scale. Huizinga states that:

> The manifestations of sorrow at the death of a prince, if at times purposely exaggerated, undoubtedly often enfolded a deep and unfeigned grief. The general instability of the soul, the extreme horror of death, the fervour of family attachment and loyalty, all contributed to make the decease of a king or a prince an afflicting event ... Noisy manifestations of sorrow were thought fine and becoming, and all things connected with a deceased person had to bear witness to an unmeasured grief.

Huizinga goes on to tell how a queen of France could not leave her room for a whole year after the death of her consort was announced and how even the princesses were secluded for six weeks. Such were the royal forms of mourning: public and extravagant. Pertelote rises to the occasion and the comedy lies in two things: first, Chauntecleer is not dead, he has only been abducted; and secondly, we smile less at the degree of the lamentation than at the inappropriateness of the comparison between this frantic chirping and the tears of some of the great ladies of antiquity.

This is the last we hear and see of Pertelote. When we first heard her speak she was the domineering, down-to-earth wife asserting her 'maistrie' through her knowledge of dream-lore and laxatives. She was the common-sense woman who refused to believe in the significance of dreams. When we leave her, she is still in error as – with all sincerity – she plays the role of the grandly mourning queen. And, besides this, we have seen her both as a loved lady from romance, as a strident wife whose husband can just keep her in her place, and as a 'type' of Eve whose bad advice 'broghte us first to wo'. It is indeed a rich presentation and the Nun's Priest's comments on his own creation make it yet richer and more various.

Russel

In some respects, Russel is the least complicated of the major characters in *The Nun's Priest's Tale*. Of course, this does not mean he is any less vividly described. Indeed, our perceptions of him range from his being a horrific figure glimpsed in a nightmare, through to his actual lurking in the Widow's yard, his wonderfully insidious speech – and, in a poem where speeches are a crucial element in the characterization, Russel's is quite as fine as any – his rough seizure of Chauntecleer by the 'gargat' and through to the point where the tables are turned on him, he loses his prey and is left grumbling and recriminating at the foot of the tree into which Chauntecleer has escaped. There is, throughout the presentation of Russel, a wonderful combination of the comic and the violently sinister. Our early analogy to *Tom and Jerry* holds up well.

But for all the poem's happy comedy, Russel is far from just a figure of fun. His appearance in the dream is so frightening that Chauntecleer groans and wakes. The cockerel leaves us in no doubt that he has seen something truly horrifying:

> I saugh a beste,
> Was lyk an hound, and wolde han maad areste
> Upon my body, and wolde han had me deed.
> His colour was bitwixe yelwe and reed;
> And tipped was his tail, and bothe his eres,
> With blak, unlyk the remenant of his heres·
> His snowte smal, with glowinge eyen tweye.
> Yet of his look for fere almost I deye;
> This caused me my groning, doutelees.

Various conventional medieval associations reinforce this idea of the fox as a symbol of some very dark forces indeed. For example, the Bestiaries – those crucial sources for the symbolic significance of animals – suggest that the fox represents the devil himself. The following translation from a thirteenth-century manuscript makes this clear:

The devil is thus like the fox with his evil slights and treachery; a man also deserves to have the fox's name for whosoever says other than good and thinks evil is a fox, a fiend.

The devil is like a fox because both are cunning tricksters. Man, when he behaves in a similar way, is like both of them. We have already seen that Boethius declared that when a man 'be a prevy awaitour y-hid and reioyseth him to ravisshe by wyles, thou shalt seyn him lyke to the fox-whelpes'. Russel, of course, as he breaks through the hedges and crouches down in the hen yard, fits this description perfectly. He is the fiend come to tempt Chauntecleer, to lure him to his destruction. Indeed, when he first actually appears – as opposed to being an image in Chauntecleer's dream – the Nun's Priest relates him to the devil by calling him a 'col fox' who is 'ful of sly iniquitee'. In other words, he is a black deceiver, the Prince of Darkness.

He has the devil's cunning too. As the Parson states: 'the devel feighteth agayns a man more by queyntise [cunning] and by sleighte than by strengthe'. And Chauntecleer, of course, is in just the state to succumb. Uxoriousness has blinded his reason to the possible warnings contained in his dream, while, with his sexual appetite slaked, he struts around his little empire, the very embodiment of Pride, Sloth, Lust and the malice that blinds the soul to seeing its errors and proper duties. And this – the 'hard-line' theological interpretation – also helps to clarify our view of Russel as the devil. Just as Chauntecleer falls into some of the Seven Deadly Sins, so the fox is motivated by them as well.

The first and most obvious point is that Russel wishes cold-bloodedly to destroy Chauntecleer. We should not allow the comedy of the Tale, its light tone and happy ending, to blind us to this fact. Russel has every intention of destroying Chauntecleer. And the will to destroy is just what characterizes the devil in traditional theology. He wishes to snatch souls to perdition, just as Russel wishes to snatch Chauntecleer off to his lair. It is quite appropriate to see Chauntecleer, as he is caught by the 'gargat' and rushed away, falling metaphorically into the mouth of hell.

But we can be somewhat more specific than this. For example, the Parson states that 'the seconde spece [species] of Envye is Ioye of other mannes harm; and that is properly lyk to the devel, that evere rejoyseth him of mannes harm'. This not only furthers the association of Russel to the devil but allies him to the second of the Seven Deadly Sins. Further, the Nun's Priest compares Russel to all 'homicydes' and, in an amusing passage of satirized rhetoric to which we shall return, relates him to Judas, Ganelon and Sinon. Homicide or manslaughter is, as the Parson makes clear, an aspect of Wrath or, as he calls it, Ire. And Ire is the third of the Seven Deadly Sins. 'Of this cursed sinne of Ire cometh eek manslaughtre,' he declares. And this is not the only aspect of the matter to which Ire contributes. We have mentioned that Russel's speech is a finely honed piece of flattery. He begins by allaying Chauntecleer's natural fear of him, declaring with what we can now see as marvellously disingenuous irony:

> Now certes, I were worse than a feend,
> If I to yow wolde harm or vileinye.

He then proceeds to flatter Chauntecleer's voice. Chauntecleer's singing is, he says, angelic. Indeed, the cockerel has more 'felinge' for music than Boethius himself who, in addition to writing on philosophy, also wrote a complex treatise of the art of music that underlies much medieval musical theory. Chauntecleer's parents are then mentioned, and the cockerel is oblivious to the warnings contained in Russel's statement that they

> Han in myn hous y-been, to my gret ese

Chauntecleer is then told that he is an even better performer than his father. Russel feigns the rapture of any opera enthusiast as he describes Chauntecleer *père*:

> He wolde so peyne him, that with bothe his yën
> He moste winke, so loude he wolde cryen,
> And stonden on his toptoon ther-with-al,
> And strecche forth his nekke long and smal.
> And eek he was of swich discrecioun,
> That ther nas no man in no regioun
> That him in song or wisdom mighte passe.

These physical details may well be fine points of the art. We know that they have a far more sinister significance. The man – or cockerel – who, in his Pride and slothful negligence, closes his eyes and so absurdly exposes himself to his enemy – the enemy of every man – is beguiled into the mouth of hell. Chauntecleer will be no exception. Finally, to cap his evident success, Russel states:

> But certeyn, ther nis no comparisoun
> Bitwix the widom and discrecioun
> Of youre fader, and of his subtiltee.

Chauntecleer, of course, is 'ravisshed with his flaterye', but the pun contained in the verb – 'ravisshe' can mean both 'overjoyed' and 'snatched away' – should alert us to the subtlety of the Nun's Priest's language. It is an example of his delight in paradox, a matter we shall discuss in the last section. Here, meanwhile, we should return to the Parson's placing flattery among the various species of Ire. He devotes a paragraph to flatterers, and what he says defines much of both Russel's nature and his effect on Chauntecleer.

Lat us now touche the vyce of flateringe, which ne comth nat gladly but for drede or for coveitise. Flaterye is generally wrongful preisinge. Flatereres been the develes norices, that norissen hise children with milk of losengerie. For sothe, Salomon seith, that 'flaterie is wors than detraccioun'. For somtyme detraccion maketh an hautein man be the more humble, for he dredeth detraccion; but certes flaterye, that maketh a man to enhauncen his herte and his contenaunce. Flatereres been the develes enchauntours; for they make a man to wene of him-self be lyk that he nis nat lyk. They been lyk to Iudas that bitraysed [god; and thise flatereres bitraysen] a man to sellen him to his enemy, that is, to the devel. Flatereres been the develes chapelleyns, that singen evere *Placebo*. I rekene flaterye in the vyces of Ire; for ofte tyme, if o man be wrooth with another, thanne wol he flatere som wight to sustene him in his querele.

drede: fear	*coveitise*: coveteousness
norices: nurses	*losengerie*: flattery
detraccioun: strife	*hautein*: haughty
bitraysed: betray	*Placebo*: I will please

But Chauntecleer escapes. He turns on the fox by using his wits. In his sinful state he has fallen victim to the subtleties of the tempter. But there is hope of salvation even to the last. Though the devil may work through 'queyntise', men, as the Parson declares, 'shal withstonden him by wit and by resoun and by discrecioun'. .

Chauntecleer, as we have seen, has these qualities in abundance. It is not grand speculation that saves him – not his pretension, his books and his learning. He survives by dint of a much more ordinary capacity. Rushing ever nearer to the mouth of hell, the teeth of the devil gripped about his throat, his wife having given him up for lost and his owner making a glorious hullabaloo in his pursuit, Chauntecleer does to the devil as the devil did to him. In the moment of Russel's triumph, Chauntecleer appeals to his vanity:

> 'sire, if that I were as ye,
> Yet sholde I seyn (as wis god helpe me),
> Turneth agayn, ye proude cherles alle!
> A verray pestilence up-on yow falle!
> Now am I come un-to this wodes syde,
> Maugree your heed, the cok shal heer abyde;
> I wil him ete in feith, and that anon.'

And without Russel even having the satisfaction of the boast – his will has consented to action and that is sufficient – Chauntecleer flutters up into a nearby tree. No amount of disingenuous pleading will bring him down. He has learnt his lesson. So has the fox.

The Widow

A delightful description of the Widow opens *The Nun's Priest's Tale* and helps provide one element of its charm. Hers is, it seems, a 'once upon a time' world. Like many such worlds, it appears idyllic at first. There is a patient, stoic healthiness about the Widow's 'ful simple lyf'. Her poverty is at one with an untroubled Christian trust, while the narrator's delight in the physical details of her existence – the 'narwe cotage', the sooty 'bour', the 'seynd bacoun' – helps to suggest a close, warm observation tinged with kindly irony. We are convinced – but we should be careful. We have suggested that *The Nun's Priest's Tale* relies for much of its effect on certain particularly medieval concepts and that its narrator enjoys a subtle sense of ambiguity. Both these elements have a part to play in the presentation of the Widow. Although the literal, historical existence of the old soul is created with convincing ease and draws our imaginative sympathy at once, we shall see that there may well be deeper levels of significance to the portrait that allow us to ally it to the shifting allegorical nature of the whole.

For example, despite the fact that by the close of the fourteenth century serfdom and the idea of fixed social classes was becoming impractical and highly contentious – we shall see why in a moment – there remained in the minds of many the ideal of an immutable order, an untroubled society of stable social estates. It was an impossible, backward-looking view in a period of turbulent social change, but its existence suggests – in terms of *The Nun's Priest's Tale* – that the initial portrait of the Widow with its image of patient poverty is far from a simple matter. The paragraph was written, we should remember, some time after the Peasants' Revolt of 1381, and this and the literature of social unrest that accompanied the Revolt is of some bearing on the portrait. Further, this picture of impoverished content is far from being the only image of the Widow that we have. When Russel invades the hen run, the whole village rises up and makes such a hullabaloo that:

> Certes, he Iakke Straw, and his meynee,
> Ne made never shoutes half so shrille,
> Whan that they wolden any Fleming kille,
> As thilke day was maad upon the fox.

Such a comparison to this traumatic event would have sent a tremor down the spine of all members of Chaucer's audience, and this helps to suggest that *The Nun's Priest's Tale* plays nimbly over some of the profound contradictions in late medieval society.

We should secure a few details of background information before we discuss this. Some elements of the static view of society – what we may again refer to as the 'hard-line' approach – draw an analogy between the poor peasant's relation to his feudal master and the soul's relation to sin and God. Just as sin puts the soul in thraldom – we have already met this idea in our application of *The Parson's Tale* to Chauntecleer – and the soul is, further, in an abject position before its creator, so it was held to be with the peasant. He or she was in servitude to a lord and was properly in the state of wholesome humility. We might turn to the teaching of Anselm of Laon at this point:

Servitude is ordained by God, either because of the sins of those who become serfs, or as a trial, in order that those who are thus humbled may be made better. For servitude is of great help to religion in protecting humility. The guardian of all virtues; and it would seem to be pride for anyone to wish to change that condition which has been given him for good reason by the divine ordinance.

In the opening paragraph of *The Nun's Priest's Tale* the Widow seems joyfully to accept such humility as is suggested here. She is fit, content and self-sufficient. She has her little dairy-farming enterprise and is quite unaware of the temptations of managerial capitalism. It does not cross her mind to expand her business and, with her new wealth, join the upwardly socially mobile. Poor she might be, but at least she is at peace. And it is this last quality that is so engaging. Humbly untroubled by money or social prestige, living by 'such as God hir sente', and a Widow at a time when, as we have seen, widowhood was regarded as a worthier estate than marriage and second in blessedness only to virginity, she is a particle of God's immemorial providence: a humble, faithful soul, an image of mankind in its best relation to the world and its maker. In this respect we should, of course, compare her to the abundantly fleshly Chauntecleer.

But in terms of fourteenth-century England, the picture of the contented Widow that is presented here was an image only of what might have once been. And when it did perhaps exist it was, in truth, an unpleasantly harsh way of life. We should look for a moment at the historical reality. It will help us, among other things, to see how accurately the Widow's environment is described.

At its strictest, feudalism meant that serfs were not free, that they tilled their lord's land, were as much a part of his property as his livestock and could not leave his estates. The very poorest – of which the Widow is not one – lived in tent-shaped hovels, while the marginally more prosperous lived in 'cruck houses', built on a solid timber framework; such houses only very rarely had chimneys or glass. Most, like the Widow's 'narwe cotage', had a couple of rooms – ironically called here the 'bour' and the 'halle' – and poultry and other animals were often kept inside. Vegetables were grown in the surrounding garden and bees were often kept as, indeed, they are by the Widow. As A. R. Nyers remarks:

Fasting in Lent was often a necessity; and after a winter passed in dark, draughty, smoky huts, living on salted beef and smoked bacon, dried peas and beans, the remains of last year's wheat or rye (or oats in the north or barley in the west), and a few winter greens, men welcomed the spring with fervent joy. Poets did not sing of autumnal splendour then; their delight was in the 'merry month of May', and the light, warmth, vitality, and freshness of spring. Fresh food was a great treat; and the lack of enough milk, butter, and cheese, especially in winter, meant that resistence to epidemics was low. The diet was also deficient in fruit and greenstuffs; fruit was thought dangerous to health, and vegetables were used mainly as seasonings for soups and meat, with the result that scurvy was prevalent, especially at the end of winter. If peasants fell ill, they relied chiefly on local women wise in the lore of herbs and other traditional remedies. Physicians were very rare in villages; but this was probably an advantage in most illnesses, in view of the constant blood-letting and queer remedies advocated by the medical lore of the time.

That Chauntecleer should be so proud in such a world makes him particularly ridiculous, while the fact that the old Widow is both so content and so spry suggests that such deprivations as hers were thought to be, when properly understood, an aid to a healthy body and a happy soul.

But they afforded no protection whatsoever against the Black Death that, between 1348 and 1379, decimated the country and helped to change its social and economic structure so profoundly that the 'hard-line' religious interpretation of the peasant's life retreated ever further into the potent world of myth. The 'hard-line' view became an ideal to hold on to in what was now a world of chronic social and economic uncertainty. A passage from a long Latin satire by Chaucer's friend John Gower shows how many men felt in the new and insecure world of social mobility and extreme proletarian revolt. He thus describes the peasantry:

who are under obligation to enter into the labours of agriculture, which are necessary for obtaining food and drink for the sustenance of the human race. After knighthood there remains only the peasant rank – the rustics in it cultivate the grain and vineyards. They are the men who seek food for us by the sweat of their heavy toil, as God Himself decreed. The guiding principle of our first father Adam, which he received from the mouth of God on high, is rightly theirs ... Now, however, scarcely a farmer wishes to do such work, and instead he wickedly loafs everywhere.

But such wicked loafing was not the only matter to frighten Gower. While we should always remember that the great chase in *The Nun's Priest's Tale* is above all things comic – in terms of the poem a superb explosion of noise after so much debate – such an activity could not but have its darker, more ambiguous side in the 1390s. These villagers may seem harmless enough, but even as we think of them actively protecting the Widow's property, so we should place this in a wider context of men and women rising up to protect what they now thought of as theirs: the wealth of the country. The Nun's Priest's comparison of the chase to the Peasants' Revolt should alert us to this – and we may care to think of other passages in Gower's *Vox Clamantis* where he describes the rioting peasantry as:

bands of rabble changed into asses, terrifying monsters, rascally bands of the common mob wandering destructively through fields in countless throngs. God's curse had changed them into irrational wild beasts whose former usefulness as tamed beasts of burden was now lost. They demanded greater delicacies, refusing to be beasts of burden, and imitated the style and dress of horses trying to aggrandise themselves with what nature had denied them.

'Law and order in nature was banished,' Gower says ominously. Then, turning to the march on London itself – that central and most dramatic episode in the Peasants' Revolt – he declares:

This was a day when everywhere the weak man terrified the strong, the humblest the noble, and the little the great. This was the day no record had previously told the likes of, if we confess the truth. A Jackdaw commonly Wat [a conflation of Wat Tyler and Jack Straw] assumed command over the other wild beasts with great rhetorical skills. Behold, the untutored heart's sense of shame was lost and it no longer feared the terrors of crime and punishment. Just as the lioness rages when robbed of her nursing cub and attacks the cattle near her, so the angry peasantry, bereft of the safeguard of justice, attacked the nobles with greater ferocity.

The Widow and the other villagers in *The Nun's Priest's Tale*, twice as 'shrille' as 'he Iakke Straw and his meynee', are a very different proposition to the 'once upon a time world' of the Widow in the opening with her grateful, patient and 'ful simple lyf'. Once again, *The Nun's Priest's Tale* shows itself to be – for all its prevailing sense of comedy – a work that is profoundly ambiguous in its contrasts and references. We should now turn to consider these more fully.

6. Rhetoric and Comic Wisdom

The Nun's Priest's Tale belongs to an oral tradition of literature, a tradition vividly illustrated on the page of an illuminated manuscript that shows Chaucer reading aloud to his courtly audience. To become a part of that audience – a necessary critical activity – we need to share a number of its preoccupations. This Introduction has tried to suggest both a few of the more ascertainable of these and to imply that their presentation is far from a straightforward matter. Some medieval interests reflected in the Tale – the problems of Pride and Lust, the ever-present menace of destruction, the nature of dreams, free will and the vigorous allure of the beast fable – remain enduring interests. Other matters, particularly the patterns of ideas through which the people of the middle ages pictured these concepts, analysed and then communicated them, are more problematic. For example, to recreate the many levels of meaning suggested by the allegorical use of animals as a part of our literary pleasure requires an agile and well-informed imagination. But for us, as we read the poem – preferably aloud and to a group of others – certain further problems inevitably present themselves. They concern rhetoric and the Nun's Priest's comic wisdom.

We have, first of all, to recreate the character of the Nun's Priest himself, and, as we have indicated, this is no simple matter. Indeed, it becomes more complex as the poem proceeds. *The General Prologue* has provided us – most unusually – with almost no clues at all. In the Prologue to the Tale itself we learn more. We are told there of the Nun's Priest's personal and vocational excellence, and we may detect from his words something of his wry and humane character. But it is in the telling of the actual Tale that his fuller complexity as a character is developed. We see there his skilful juxtaposition of apparently contradictory attitudes, the often kind and wise irony of which is then further developed in asides and interjections, until, in the closing section of the poem, we realize that we are dealing with a created character of the utmost literary sophistication. We shall have to develop these ideas, but should pause here to question the implications of what we have already said.

It will be obvious that, in searching for a tone of voice and perhaps even gestures and facial expressions for our reading, we are faced with similar problems to those that confront an actor. The text before us is something we are called upon to interpret in a remarkably comprehensive way. Precisely because *The Nun's Priest's Tale* is a poem in an oral tradition and exploits the full range of possibilities presented in that tradition by having the narrator a highly complex character in his own right, there is no place in the Tale itself for explicit authorial guidance on what is a most beguiling presentation. We have here the engaging illusion that the speaker is himself the author of his Tale and that he creates his persona in the process of revealing his art. Of course, there is a further level to this illusion: the Nun's Priest, self-creating although he appears to be, is actually a creation of Chaucer the poet's – and not Chaucer the pilgrim's – art. Nonetheless, the interpretative problem remains: How are we, reading Chaucer's words, to create a satisfactory picture of a character who appears wholly self-created in the act of telling his Tale?

The obvious analogy that springs to mind, as we have said, is that of the stage actor. But Shakespeare himself appears in *Hamlet* more or less only in so far as he has created a comprehensible structure in which the actor must interpret the nuances by which the Prince is to be given life. We are given no explicit guidance. And who has ever seen two identical Hamlets? Any number of the aspects of his character – the elements of his creation – may be stressed to complement and modify others. Within the constraints of the text – a matter of no small significance – Hamlet is protean. Of course, there are further factors. The reactions of other characters define him and the director's interpretation will shape both these and the initial conception of the hero. But in reading *The Nun's Priest's Tale* there *are* really no other characters and we have to be our own directors as well. We are presented with what we may loosely call an extended soliloquy and we have to judge for ourselves precisely the degree of irony behind the rhetorical apostrophes, while – perhaps even more problematic – we also have to work out how we are going to deliver a line such as:

I can noon harm of no womman divyne.

Is the emphasis resolutely on the first syllable, and, if it is, what does this suggest about the Nun's Priest's extra-textual experience of women? How far should our tone of voice suggest that this is a relevant concern at all? Or is the declaration perhaps – and a body of criticism has built up around this possibility – directed to the Prioress? If this is so, is it said in a subservient way, a subservient way that – to us at least – implies irony. Or is it polite, even friendly? And then again, there is the problem of precisely what the line may mean. Does it mean that the Nun's Priest can 'divyne' no harm in women, or does it mean that he can find no harm in women who are divine? The difference is an important one. Both meanings may well be present. This is a further example of the ambiguity and paradox that characterize the Nun's Priest's subtle intelligence and add to the problems of those who would speak the poem aloud. Much of this ambiguity we can obviously never resolve. We do not have Chaucer's own reading to act as a standard, and so our uncertainty lands us in the position where we are free to try the full range of interpretation that our imaginative rediscovery of the text can reasonably bear. In a poem as rich as this, we must always face the protean nature of interpretation.

In addition to the problems involved in creating a satisfactory characterization of a master storyteller from his own words, we also have the analogous problem of interpreting his fictional devices. These we need to discuss under two heads: first, that of the sensations he may be trying to produce in his audience, and secondly the tone of voice by which these are to be achieved. We may take the opening paragraph as an example.

We have commented already on the opening's regard for concrete detail. Whatever else it is – and it can be many things – the portrait of the Widow is closely observed. But the humour here is already complex, for there is a mockery of the high-flown in the opening paragraph that is crucial to the tone of the rest of the text. The Nun's Priest talks of the Widow's 'bour, and eek her halle'. Peasants actually lived in hovels – 'poor pelting cottages' as Shakespeare called them – and there is no reason to think that this one is any different. What, then, is the precise effect of the humour here? Is there a mildly unkind suggestion of satire in the vocabulary? Probably not. Is there simply a genial sense of irony? Probably so. However, there are additional aspects of literary effect in this instance which are at once obvious to a modern audience and were of particular significance to a medieval one. There is, for example, a story-book quality about the description of the Widow, a sense of never-never-land. The Widow belongs with other characters such as the Old Woman who lived in a Shoe, and the widows of folk-tale, many of whom, perhaps like her, are nowhere near as safely virtuous as they may at first seem to be. However, we will set that particular ambiguity aside for a moment and concentrate instead on the humanity of the initial presentation. The Widow may well have a never-never quality about her, but, miraculously, she is not some sentimental creature out of popular children's fiction. There is here dignity that is achieved through the recognition of physical hardship and of her patience, trust and healthy content in a world of everyday physical things. As we have seen, however, such an apparently innocuous portrait is charged with political and social significances of the greatest power. All at first appears so safe, so good, so tranquil. However, to a medieval courtly audience living in the historical context of the Peasants' Revolt, this picture of an ideal and fixed social order would have been particularly potent; while, in the more narrow but precise context of a medieval audience hearing this description as part of a work of poetry, it would have inevitably prompted certain literary questions. With an audience aware, perhaps, of the polarization that Gower had shown between the ideal, fixed, happy social estates and the reality – and aware, too, of a range of political poetry and poetry of social discontent in which the ideal image of the peasant and the image of the peasant troubled or in revolt was the means of a very immediate and often satiric inquiry into the state of the nation – questions would inevitably have been triggered about what type of poem this was going to be. Was it to be a political allegory, for example, and, if so, whose side was the Nun's Priest to be on? What is going to happen to the Widow? What does she represent? And, to revert to our problem of voice, how can this help answer these questions even while they are being raised? How far, for example, is the Nun's Priest to offset the loving observation by an emphasis on such words as 'pacience', 'namo', '*hir* neded never a deel' and so on; emphases that would draw an implicit comparison between her and others who – in terms of a largely conservative and courtly audience at any rate – were far from being so apparently virtuous.

What we have here is a foretaste of that playing with literary expectation which characterizes the poem as a whole. Let us explore this idea in more detail. We long to give allegorical, social and political significance to what we have heard in the initial description of the Widow. All sorts of clues have suggested what such an interpretation might contain, and they appear to be essentially benevolent. Although she now disappears for several hundred lines, the Widow, of course, does eventually come back, and when she re-emerges it is a far from simple matter. By now, the village has been roused to protect her property, and, in terms of literary effect, there is a sheer delightful sense of release in all the noise that is made. Further, with what loving detail it is all described: the dogs, the ducks, Malkin with her distaff and the other peasants with their trumpets on which they 'pouped ... shryked and ... houped'. Here is wonderful riot of energy. But it *is* a riot. For all our pleasure, there are the most sinister undertones. The peasants 'yelleden as feendes doon in helle', and, of course, they are explicitly compared to Jack Straw, the peasants' march on London and the ensuing racial blood bath in which immigrant Flemish workers were murdered. We are back in the world of political poetry with a vengeance. But we do not stay there. The focus, intense though it has been, suddenly returns to Chauntecleer, and, interestingly, to his use of the noise the Widow and her friends are making to free himself. Their hullabaloo, for all its deeper implications, produces nothing of its own accord. It remains an allusion only, an allusion that takes its place beside other and apparently contradictory ones in the poem and thereby serves to broaden the range of reference and subvert a coherent interpretation. Expectations are raised, then, but answers are not provided. Such literary playfulness is a key to the functioning of the whole poem.

Nowhere is this literary playfulness more wittily or delightfully evident than in the presentation of Chauntecleer himself.

In our description both of Chauntecleer himself and of the intellectual concerns that lie behind him, we brought to light a number of ideas that we characterized as particularly medieval, some of which we then further delineated as 'hard-line'. We saw, for instance, that a sermon or homily in the form of a beast fable was regarded as having an explicit allegorical content and that animals could be seen both as impersonations of aspects of God's wisdom and as symbols of the bestial nature of fallen man. We saw that the apparent allegorical interest of *The Nun's Priest's Tale* itself suggests that Chauntecleer could be seen as an allegory both certain of the Seven Deadly Sins – Pride in particular – while he could also, through the 'hard-line' interpretation of the place of sexuality in marriage, be seen as a 'type' of Adam and hence of every man. He ignores a direct prompting from God and, instead, in an excess of uxorious passion, allows his senses to get the better of his reason and so pervert his will in the direction of mortal error. We saw that from this descent into sin Chauntecleer fell into Pride and the vainglory that leads to his seizure by the fox. And we saw that the fox himself was a well-recognized 'type' of the devil. Russel's jaws can be seen quite properly as the mouth of hell and his lair – which Chauntecleer never reaches – as a 'type' of the bottomless pit. We can therefore say that the allegorical narrative structure of *The Nun's Priest's Tale* derives its coherence from a clear and well-established tradition of popular teaching. It is the structure that we might well expect from a priest, particularly in a period when, as we have seen, sermons on one or more of the Seven Deadly Sins were commonplace. In this respect, *The Nun's Priest's Tale* is not radically different from the charming exemplum about the adder and the elephant cited on p. 28.

But, of course, it is evident that such a comparison goes nowhere to suggesting the fullness of our response to *The Nun's Priest's Tale*. It is not a mechanical – if beguiling – homily. Indeed, as we have suggested, it is a most complex work of art in which conventional, traditional expectations are consistently thwarted. Having through an effort of scholarship aspired to become more or less ideal members of the original audience, we can bring conventional expectations to what we hear, but, unless we are also prepared to be very flexible with these, to have them raised, tested and perhaps rejected, then we shall miss both a great deal of the humour and, finally, the exhilarating freedom of Chaucer's comic intelligence.

In an often quoted phrase, the novelist D. H. Lawrence urged the reader to trust the tale and not the teller. In *The Nun's Priest's Tale* Chaucer is asking us to do the reverse. We are asked to understand the conventional associations which the ecclesiastical use of the popular story of the cock and the fox would suggest – in other words the implications of the 'hard-line' ideas underlying it – but, through the increasingly ebullient self-revelation of the character of the fictional narrator, we are also asked to at least give an ear to the teller of the tale and admit the subsequent possibility of refusing to give implicit trust to the conventional expectations his tale arouses. It is to achieve this mode of criticism that Chaucer has carefully created the Nun's Priest's personality through asides in which, either implicitly or directly, he subverts his own conventional teaching.

For example, the marriage of Chauntecleer presents us with a wealth of simultaneous but contradictory assertions. Officially, the church did not approve of courtly love. Such passion placed too much emphasis on human emotion without a concomitant wish to conceive children and so was reckoned to divert the mind from its proper duties to God. Yet, as we have seen, courtly love was a most civilizing force in Western Europe, and it is clear from *The Nun's Priest's Tale* itself that the narrator is affected by its idealism. It is, paradoxically, partly through the vocabulary of aristocratic passion that Chauntecleer the cockerel becomes most touchingly human. Again, as we have also seen, an over-emphasis on sexual passion even in marriage was regarded as sinful. The Nun's Priest, on the other hand, suggests that sexuality is an exuberant delight – an implication that will later earn the ribald comments of the Host – while at the same time he tells a story whose allegorical narrative depends precisely on the fact that such indulgence is not only sinful and dangerous but is an imitation of the primal error of Adam, an error which not only brought sin into the world but which triggered the whole vast and complicated process of the death and resurrection of the incarnated Christ and the promise of the eventual salvation of man. In *The Parson's Tale* the nature and variety of sin, the corruption of man, the foolish state of worldly Pride and the worthlessness of mere human existence are all emphasized with a dreadful thoroughness. The only and proper dignity of man is a state of servitude, patience and contrition. And yet the Nun's Priest refuses to be borne along on this traditional groundswell of self-disgust. He constantly rises above it to reaffirm the delightfulness of living even while he tells a story whose apparent symbolic import denies it. Contrary views are expressed in the tale. One view – the 'hard-line' one – is implied, largely silent and to be grasped in the main by our knowledge of medieval preoccupations. The other view is largely explicit and arises from the Nun's Priest's tone of evident relish in Chauntecleer's sensual, proud delights.

And this is just the paradox unwittingly posed by Chauntecleer himself at the crucial moment when, having re-established his 'maistrie', he immediately loses it in his uxorious passion for his wife. His dream, as we have seen, may fairly be interpreted as a warning from God. It is prefigurative, admonitory. Chauntecleer at first accepts it as such. Then, suddenly, he rejects the warning. He looks on Pertelote's beauty, abandons his reason and then tries to justify his decision through the scholarship that had previously helped him towards a knowledge of the truth. It is a delightful irony. Overcome by female charm, he mistranslates his boastful Latin:

> *In principio,*
> *Mulier est hominis confusio;*
> Madame, the sentence of this Latin is –
> Womman is mannes Ioye and al his blis.

It is not nearly enough to see this mistranslation as a mere 'schoolboy howler' on Chauntecleer's part. His mistranslation is both an error and a profound truth. It is right – according to 'hard-line' theology – that woman brought man to confusion. It is also right – in purely human and loving terms – that 'womman is mannes Ioye and al his blis'. The paradox is a condition of life in the sublunary world. And, in asserting this paradox, the growing force of the Nun's Priest's personality develops until he becomes so profoundly involved against the morality of the tale he tells – a morality based on 'hard-line' theology – that the idea of fiction itself becomes tested.

This becomes particularly apparent in the paragraph beginning at l. 367 which opens, as we have seen, with the fallen Chauntecleer telling the time from the stars. We should note that these are no longer seen as the means by which divine admonitions are received. They now serve a purely worldly and functional end for this noble intellectual strutting vain-gloriously across the dunghill earth, or – the other side of the continuing paradox – strolling satisfied through his garden of love in a state of human content. Such bliss cannot last. We know it cannot. But any statement to this effect is bound to look intolerably crass. The Nun's Priest is perfectly well aware of this and so at once sets up and parodies the rhetoric of the 'Fall of Princes' genre – the genre to which his own Tale, in some ways, belongs:

> But sodeinly him fil a sorweful cas;
> For ever the latter ende of Ioye is wo.
> God woot that worldly Ioye is sone ago;
> And if a rethor coude faire endyte,

> He in a cronique saufly mighte it wryte,
> As for a sovereyn notabilitee.

rethor: rhetorician   *endyte*: compose, set down

Surely we are meant to smile at this self-conscious banality. But, once again, there is a paradox. On the one hand the ideas behind what the Nun's Priest says are true. We have seen that the wheel of Fortune was a dominant image in the medieval mind; while, on the other hand, the facts of the ups and downs of life are so banal that dwelling on them becomes almost futile. The Nun's Priest has here both set up the mechanism of the 'Fall of Princes' genre and mocked it at the same time.

But his parody and interjection here also achieve something else. The Nun's Priest frees us from the necessity of having to give our imaginative consent to the plot of his Tale. He has already stretched the possibilities of the beast fable to their fullest extent. Our willed suspension of disbelief has been tested to the utmost. Now the ground is suddenly pulled from under us. We are told:

> This storie is al-so trewe, I undertake,
> As is the book of Launcelot de Lake,
> That wommen holde in ful gret reverence.

In other words the Nun's Priest declares the narrative content of his Tale to be nothing more than a frivolous fiction. Nonetheless, with superb irony, he goes on to complete his Tale, and to complete it with an ever-increasing wealth of personal comment, intellectual reference and formal satire.

It is particularly adroit in this context that, in turning again to his 'sentence', what the Nun's Priest first does is to take us straight back into the storyland world of his poem with his compelling description of Russel. No sooner has he done so, however, than he alternates this with a further passage of ironic rhetoric. Russel, crouching down to wait for Chauntecleer, is compared to the great traitors of the past, to Judas, Ganelon and Sinon. The allegorical thread continues to be spun. The evil of Russel's intentions is given a moral context. But the emphasis has changed. The comic excess of the comparisons now makes us smile.

What then follows is the discussion of Fortune. It is, perhaps, the most dexterous passage in the whole poem and the one in which conventional rhetorical associations are the most acutely parodied. The tone of lamentation has been both set up and sent up. The great traitors of the past – and, by implication, the great men they destroyed – have been compared to the forthcoming farmyard tussle between Russel the devil and Chauntecleer the Prince. There then follows the apostrophe to

Chauntecleer. He has been forewarned in dreams 'that thilke day was perilous', but – so the narrator, playing with the traditional rhetoric of the 'Fall of Princes' genre, would have us believe – a ruthless, divine determinism now ensures his destruction. In fact, of course, it does no such thing. Chauntecleer, as we know, escapes. However, to set the initial effect of this passage – ll. 410–15 – in context, we may refer to the closing stanza of *The Monk's Tale* of which, as we have seen, *The Nun's Priest's Tale* serves as a criticism. In the last of the Monk's stories, Croesus has also been warned in a dream of his forthcoming death. Nonetheless

> Anhanged was Cresus, the proude king,
> His royal trone mighte him nat availle. –
> Tragedie is noon other maner thing,
> Ne can in singing crye ne biwaille,
> But for that fortune alwey wol assaille
> With unwar strook the regnes that ben proude;
> For when men trusteth hir, than wol she faille,
> And covere hir brighte face with a cloude.

trone: throne   *regnes*: kings

It is this sort of thing that bores the Knight and the Host and which *The Nun's Priest's Tale* parodies: the dreary rhetoric, the doom-laden pomposity, the unquestioning acceptance of disaster. But what the lively mind of the Nun's Priest also objects to is the philosophical naïvety. In *The Monk's Tale* Fortune is a largely untested abstraction, and the Nun's Priest will have none of it. He knows that the issue of Fortune is a very complex one. He sets up the rhetoric of a weak-minded acceptance of determinism, and then – with an adroitness characteristic of his whole approach – subverts it. Fortune – the evil genius of the 'Fall of Princes' genre – is not nearly as simple as its rhetorical forms would imply. Indeed, Fortune is a major philosophical problem which had occupied some of the liveliest minds. As a result, far from being an agreed entity, it was the subject of 'gret altercacioun ... and greet disputisoun'. Intelligence and knowledge of current philosophical development undermine the rhetorical cliché and so destroy the easy forms of the 'Fall of Princes' genre as employed by the Monk. Once again – and this time in full view of the audience – the machinery of literary expectation has been set up only to be immediately dismantled by a shrewd comic intelligence.

And, having done this, the narrator then proceeds to set up and dismantle the appropriate rhetoric for his presentation of Pertelote as a type of Eve. The clichés of anti-feminism are trotted out. That they are clichés is suggested by the Nun's Priest's saying that if we want to read this sort of thing then we had better go and consult other 'auctours, wher they trete of swich matere' and by the Nun's Priest's own appreciation of women. His own perceptions contradict the conventions implicit in the 'hardline' approach to women. By the richest of ironies, Chaucer the poet has a priest jokingly set up the clichés of ecclesiastical anti-feminism only to undermine them by a personal – and, in its full extent, forbidden – appreciation of 'womman divyne'.

Explicit literary parody now becomes the subject of the poem: its medium and its message. The abduction of Chauntecleer has taken place. The Prince has been seized. He is being hurried away to hell itself. Death and destruction are imminent. An appropriate rhetoric is required, and it comes to hand through one of the most popular rhetorical manuals of the middle ages: the *Poetria Nova* of Geoffrey de Vinsauf. This book was almost certainly familiar to Chaucer – he uses it in *Troilus and Criseyde* – but the particular passage he refers to, the lamentation on the death of Richard the Lionheart, was also circulated independently. It is this that the Nun's Priest parodies here.

De Vinsauf's work is a serious, scholarly attempt to re-express some of the rhetorical formulas derived from the classical world in terms of medieval preoccupations. It is detailed and helpful but poetically inert. Though the book deals briefly with humour – saying that the comic is best expressed through the colloquial, as, indeed, it is in *The Nun's Priest's Tale* – Chaucer evidently saw the comic possibilities opened up first by an application of 'high' rhetoric to his 'low' subject matter, and secondly in the somewhat humourless pomp of Geoffrey's attempt at an elegy for King Richard. He plays with great delight on the astrology in de Vinsauf's piece – its emphasis on the fact that Friday made the death so particularly unlucky, Friday, the tearful day of Venus, planet of love, whose day became night, and so on and so on:

> O Veneris lacrimosa dies! O sidus amarum!
> Illa dies tua nox fuit et Venus illa venerum.

This is woeful stuff indeed, though we should note how the parody neatly returns us to the lustful Chauntecleer, the servant of Venus who has placed sex before procreation. Even in the satire the serious issues are not forgotten. But, having twitted Geoffrey de Vinsauf and said that he himself is unable to lavish comparable skills on his subject, the Nun's Priest creates that superb paragraph of parody in which the frantically clucking Pertelote is compared to the great widows of antiquity. The paragraph is, as is typical of the technique of the whole poem, wonderfully satirized by its concluding line. Once more we are consciously beguiled by the artifice and made aware the *The Nun's Priest's Tale* sets up rhetorical expectations only to subvert them.

This is equally true of the conclusion to *The Nun's Priest's Tale*. Having developed his material to an unprecedented degree, the Nun's Priest has, to abide by the literary rules, to point out the 'moralitee' of what he has been saying. What he declares to his audience is this:

> Lo, swich it is for to be recchelees
> And necligent, and truste on flaterye.

Such, then, are the explicit lessons to be drawn from his sermon. They are, of course, wholly appropriate, but it is also clear that they in no way correspond to the full complexity of his utterance. The 'moralitee' is justified only in terms of the simplest level of narrative. It is what we might expect from Aesop. The full truth is more complex. The moral awareness that has been raised is far more comprehensive than the 'moralitee' that is cited. However, just before the conventional prayer that concludes the sermon, the Nun's Priest, in a final literary ploy, bids us to take the 'fruyt' that his Tale offers. Fruit is a resonant word. It is meant, perhaps, to remind us of Adam's fall. But it also suggests both the intellectual richness and the sensuality of the poem itself. Our enjoyment of the Tale is, after all, part of its meaning. To do justice to the poem we need to hold both its shifting morality and its sensuality before us. In other words, we are asked to become critics:

> ye that holden this tale a folye,
> As of a fox, or of a cok and hen,
> Taketh the moralitee, good men.
> For seint Paul seith, that al that writen is,
> To our doctryne it is y-write, y-wis.
> Taketh the fruyt, and lat the chaf be stille.

It is just the complexity of this process that this Introduction has tried to explain.

The Text, with Notes

Cresus.

This riche Cresus, whylom king of Lyde,
Of whiche Cresus Cyrus sore him dradde,
Yit was he caught amiddes al his pryde,
And to be brent men to the fyr him ladde.
But swich a reyn doun fro the welkne shadde
That slow the fyr, and made him to escape;
But to be war no grace yet he hadde,
Til fortune on the galwes made him gape.

Whan he escaped was, he can nat stente
For to biginne a newe werre agayn.   10
He wende wel, for that fortune him sente
Swich hap, that he escaped thurgh the rayn,
That of his foos he mighte nat be slayn;
And eek a sweven up-on a night he mette,
Of which he was so proud and eek so fayn,
That in vengeaunce he al his herte sette.

Up-on a tree he was, as that him thoughte,
Ther Iuppiter him wesh, bothe bak and syde,
And Phebus eek a fair towaille him broughte
To drye him with, and ther-for wex his pryde;   20
And to his doghter, that stood him bisyde,
Which that he knew in heigh science habounde,
He bad hir telle him what it signifyde,
And she his dreem bigan right thus expounde.

'The tree,' quod she, 'the galwes is to mene,
And Iuppiter bitokneth snow and reyn,
And Phebus, with his towaille so clene,
Tho ben the sonne stremes for to seyn;
Thou shalt anhanged be, fader, certeyn;
Reyn shal thee wasshe, and sonne shal thee drye;'   30
Thus warned she him ful plat and ful pleyn,
His doughter, which that called was Phanye.

1 *This riche Cresus* ...: Croesus, the richest man in the world, was defeated by the Persians under Cyrus in 546 BC. Chaucer's source for his tragic end (which is not classical) derives ultimately from a great medieval encyclopedia, the *Speculum historiale* of Vincent of Beauvais. This version of the story is also found in the *Roman de la Rose* (see Introduction, pp. 13–14), and is cited in *The Nun's Priest's Tale*, ll. 318–20.

2 *hym dradde*: feared for himself.

7 *But to be war*: but he still did not have the grace (i.e. divine favour) to be cautious.

14 *And eek a sweven* ...: the dream is, of course, cited by Chauntecleer as proof of the validity of dreams at l. 318.

Anhanged was Cresus, the proude king,
His royal trone mighte him nat availle. –
Tragedie is noon other maner thing,
Ne can in singing crye ne biwaille,
But for that fortune alwey wol assaille
With unwar strook the regnes that ben proude;
For when men trusteth hir, than wol she faille,
And covere hir brighte face with a cloude.   40

Here stinteth the Knight the Monk of his Tale.

35   *Tragedie ...*: for a discussion of the nature of tragedy and the 'Fall of Princes' genre, see Introduction, pp. 29–30.

The prologue of the Nonne Preestes Tale

'Ho!' quod the knight, 'good sir, na-more of this,
That ye han seyd is right y-nough, y-wis,
And mochel more; for litel hevinesse
Is right y-nough to mochel folk, I gesse.
I seye for me, it is a greet disese
Wher-as men han ben in greet welthe and ese,
To heren of hir sodeyn fal, allas!
And the contrarie is Ioie and greet solas,
As whan a man hath been in povre estaat,
And clymbeth up, and wexeth fortunat,   10
And ther abydeth in prosperitee,
Swich thing is gladsom, as it thinketh me,
And of swich thing were goodly for to telle.'
'Ye,' quod our hoste, 'by seint Poules belle,
Ye seye right sooth; this monk, he clappeth loude,
He spak how "fortune covered with a cloude"
I noot never what, and als of a "Tragedie"
Right now ye herde, and parde! no remedie
It is for to biwaille, ne compleyne
That that is doon, and als it is a peyne,   20
As ye han seyd, to here of hevinesse.
Sir monk, na-more of this, so god yow blesse!
Your tale anoyeth al this companye;
Swich talking is nat worth a boterflye;
For ther-in is ther no desport ne game.
Wherfor, sir Monk, or dan Piers by your name,
I preye yow hertely, telle us somwhat elles,
For sikerly, nere clinking of your belles,
That on your brydel hange on every syde,
By heven king, that for us alle dyde,   30

1   *'Ho!' quod the knight ...*: although Harry Bailey, the host, is the self-appointed arbiter of the storytelling (see Introduction, pp. 16–21), it is appropriate that the Knight should interrupt the Monk here since both are men of high social standing. For a discussion of *The Monk's Tale*, see Introduction, pp. 29–30. The word 'ho' is colloquial but was also a knightly term used to separate participants in a tournament.

2   *That ye han seyd ...*: 'what you have said is quite enough, indeed, and more than enough, for a little sadness is quite sufficient for many people, I'm sure.'

5   *I seye for me*: 'for my part'.

14 *seint Poules belle*: the bell of old St Paul's Cathedral. St Paul's was a civic centre in medieval London and its bell, which could be heard across the much smaller medieval city, summoned the citizens to assemblies. Harry Bailey would have been very familiar with its sound.

15 *clappeth*: this appropriately picks up the idea of the loud, monotonous tolling of a bell and transfers it to the Monk's storytelling. For the full implications of the bell imagery, see Introduction, pp. 30–31.

16 *He spak how ...*: Harry Bailey quotes from the Monk's definition of tragedy given at the close of the tale of Croesus. Not all manuscripts of the Prologue to *The Nun's Priest's Tale* contain ll. 5–24. It has been suggested that Chaucer inserted them later when he had also decided that the story of Croesus should be the last the Monk should tell. Previously four other stories followed it. This series of rearrangements certainly allows for the lively and satirical interchange here and helps prepare for the more colloquial tone of *The Nun's Priest's Tale*.

Harry Bailey here pretends not to understand the Monk's prescription for tragedy, from which he quotes, and his sarcasm makes his syntax difficult to follow. We might paraphrase thus: 'Yes,' said our host, 'by St Paul's bell, what you say is quite right. This monk prattles on. He spoke of "fortune covered with a cloud" – and I know not what – and just now you heard of a "tragedy". Yet, by the Lord, it's no good crying and moaning about what's done. And, what's more, it's uncomfortable [the modern colloquial form 'it's a pain' fits well here], as you [the Knight] have said, to hear of depressing matters.'

25 *desport ne game*: for a discussion of the requirement to provide pleasure or instruction, see Introduction, pp. 20–21.

28 *nere clinking of your belles*: these are the bells on the Monk's bridle. They are mentioned, along with many other significant details, in the Monk's portrait in *The General Prologue*. For a discussion of this, see Introduction, pp. 30–32.

I sholde er this han fallen doun for slepe,
Although the slough had never been so depe;
Than had your tale al be told in vayn.
For certeinly, as that thise clerkes seyn,
"Wher-as a man may have noon audience,
Noght helpeth it to tellen his sentence."
And wel I woot the substance is in me,
If any thing shal wel reported be.
Sir, sey somwhat of hunting, I yow preye.'
'Nay,' quod this monk, 'I have no lust to pleye;   40
Now let another telle, as I have told.'
Than spak our host, with rude speche and bold,
And seyde un-to the Nonnes Preest anon,
'Com neer, thou preest, com hider, thou sir Iohn,
Tel us swich thing as may our hertes glade,
Be blythe, though thou ryde up-on a Iade.
What though thyn hors be bothe foule and lene,
If he wol serve thee, rekke nat a bene;
Look that thyn herte be mery evermo.'
'Yis, sir,' quod he, 'yis, host, so mote I go,   50
But I be mery, y-wis, I wol be blamed:' –
And right anon his tale he hath attamed,
And thus he seyde un-to us everichon,
This swete preest, this goodly man, sir Iohn.

31 *fallen doun for slepe*: an obvious expression of extreme boredom. That it is also an ironic comment on *The Monk's Tale*, see Introduction, pp. 30–31.

34 *thise clerkes*: the learned generally.

35 *"Wher-as a man …*: this is a translation from the Vulgate (or Latin) Bible and may be rendered as: 'When there is no one to listen to a man's story there is no point in his speaking his wisdom.' In part this relates to the techniques of preaching good sermons, for which see Introduction, pp. 35–8.

37 *the substance is in me …*: 'I know that I have the makings (of a good listener) if a story is well told.'

39 *hunting*: the Monk is a great hunter (see Introduction, p. 30) and the Host's comment is ironic.

40 *'Nay,' quod this monk*: Piers, not surprisingly, is crushed.

43 *the Nonnes Preest*: for a discussion of the Nun's Priest's status, character and presentation, see Introduction, pp. 29–51 and 83–94.

44 *neer*: nearer.
    sir Iohn: priests were entitled to have 'sir' put before their first names, but John was a conventional priestly nickname.

46 *Iade*: for a discussion of the Nun's Priest's poor horse, see Introduction, p. 32.

48 *rekke nat a bene*: 'do not worry at all'. The theme of happy poverty is first suggested here.

50 *'Yis, sir,' quod he …*:'Yes, sir,' he said, 'yes, Host, so must I go on, for unless I tell a merry story, I will be criticized.' Note: 'go' has here the sense of 'walk' or 'ride' with, as the Host says, a happy heart. 'But' means 'unless'.

The Nonne Preestes Tale

Here biginneth the Nonne Preestes Tale of the Cok and Hen, Chauntecleer and Pertelote.

A povre widwe, somdel stape in age,
Was whylom dwelling in a narwe cotage,
Bisyde a grove, stonding in a dale.
This widwe, of which I telle yow my tale,
Sin thilke day that she was last a wyf,
In pacience ladde a ful simple lyf,
For litel was hir catel and hir rente;
By housbondrye, of such as God hir sente,
She fond hir-self, and eek hir doghtren two.
Three large sowes hadde she, and namo,   10
Three kyn, and eek a sheep that highte Malle.
Ful sooty was hir bour, and eek hir halle,
In which she eet ful many a sclendre meel.
Of poynaunt sauce hir neded never a deel.
No deyntee morsel passed thurgh hir throte;
Hir dyete was accordant to hir cote.
Repleccioun ne made hir never syk;
Attempree dyete was al hir phisyk,
And exercyse, and hertes suffisaunce.
The goute lette hir no-thing for to daunce,   20
Napoplexye shente nat hir heed;
No wyn ne drank she, neither whyt ne reed;
Hir bord was served most with whyt and blak,
Milk and broun breed, in which she fond no lak,
Seynd bacoun, and somtyme an ey or tweye,
For she was as it were a maner deye.
  A yerd she hadde, enclosed al aboute
With stikkes, and a drye dich with-oute,
In which she hadde a cok, hight Chauntecleer,
In al the land of crowing nas his peer.   30
His vois was merier than the mery orgon
On messe-dayes that in the chirche gon;

1   *A povre widwe* ...: No reader can fail to be impressed by the vivid tone of the opening paragraph. It is this that remains with us to give life to the layers of allusion which the portrait in fact possesses. These – and the contrast to ll. 555–81 – are discussed in the Introduction, pp. 80–87. It is on this level of immediacy that the contrasts between the Widow and her chicken are particularly comic and effective.

3   *Bisyde a grove* ...: this is the haunt of the fox.

5   *last a wyf*: since her husband died. We need not assume she had had more than one. For a discussion of marriage and widowhood, see Introduction, pp. 55–60.

7   *hir catel and hir rente*: property and income. 'Catel' is 'goods and chattels'. The tone is mildly ironic.

8   *By housbondrye* ...: 'by careful management of such things as God sent her she provided for herself and her two daughters'.

12   *bour* ... *halle*: bedroom and living room. Again, the tone is ironic, the words having aristocratic associations of castle life quite inappropriate for a two-room cottage. For a discussion of the cottage and medieval village life, see Introduction, pp. 81–2

16   *dyete*: her normal food.
     cote: cottage.

20   *goute*: gout – a result of an unhealthy diet – did not prevent her from dancing.

22   *whyt ne reed*: neither red nor white wine.

23   *whyt and blak*: milk and rye bread, as the next line suggests.

26   *a maner deye*: a kind of dairy maid. Note the easy, colloquial tone.

27   *A yerd she hadde*: this is Chauntecleer's empire. For the iconographic significance of the yard, see Introduction, pp. 54–5.

30   *peer*: equal.

31   *orgon*: the use of *gon* in the next line shows that the noun is plural.

32   *messe-dayes*: feast days.

Wel sikerer was his crowing in his logge,
Than is a clokke, or an abbey orlogge.
By nature knew he ech ascencioun
Of equinoxial in thilke toun;
For whan degrees fiftene were ascended,
Thanne crew he, that it mighte nat ben amended.
His comb was redder than the fyn coral,
And batailed, as it were a castel-wal.   40
His bile was blak, and as the leet it shoon;
Lyk asur were his legges, and his toon;
His nayles whytter than the lilie flour,
And lyk the burned gold was his colour.
This gentil cok hadde in his governaunce
Sevene hennes, for to doon al his plesaunce,
Whiche were his sustres and his paramours,
And wonder lyk to him, as of colours.
Of whiche the faireste hewed on hir throte
Was cleped faire damoysele Pertelote.   50
Curteys she was, discreet, and debonaire,
And compaignable, and bar hir-self so faire,
Sin thilke day that she was seven night old,
That trewely she hath the herte in hold
Of Chauntecleer loken in every lith;
He loved hir so, that wel was him therwith.

33 *logge*: perch. This is in the widow's 'halle'. The sentence may be rendered: 'His crowing from his perch was more reliable than a clock or abbey timepiece,' i.e. any clock. Chauntecleer's perch is likened to a belfrey.

35 *nature*: instinct. We have seen the significance of this (Introduction, pp. 53–4). The ability of cockerels to tell time by the light had been known from ancient times and is a matter of common observation. It is an interesting but anachronistic point of detail that a cockerel's actual and acute sensitivity to fine variations of light is affected by its pituitary gland, which controls the development of sexual maturity and egg production. See note to l. 341.

35–6 *ascencioun ... equinoxial ...*: we pass to more important matters of medieval science, in which Chaucer was deeply interested. The passage tells us that Chauntecleer crew every hour. The 'equinoxial' was an imaginary circle drawn round the heavens, of which the earth was believed to be the centre. A point on the circumference of the 'equinoxial', moving from east to west, completed the circle of 360° in twenty-four hours. It follows that one hour represents $\frac{360°}{24}$ or 15°. Chauntecleer could tell when each one of 15° was about to appear above the horizon. In other words he knew that an hour had passed and crew to record the fact. Obviously, the rising or 'ascencioun' of each of these divisions varied according to the longitude of the observer and therefore what Chauntecleer recorded was 'local time', the 'ascencioun' of 15° as it was observed 'in thilke toun', i.e. in his own village.

45 *gentil*: of high birth and breeding (compare the widow).

46 *Sevene*: it is perhaps worth pointing out that seven is more or less the recommended size for the smallest domestic chicken flock and so points to the widow's poverty and why she could only spare 'somtyme an ey or tweye'.

47 *his sustres and his paramours*: such bluntly physical detail reminds us to be very careful when reading the story too humourlessly as an allegory. Whatever else the author may certainly suggest, Chauntecleer is firmly the cock of this particular walk, and his pursuit of 'plesaunce' will lead to his near downfall.

50 *damoysele*: lady. The tone is again ironic. For an analysis of Pertelote, see Introduction, pp. 73–5. Note how the adjectives Chaucer uses to describe her further suggest the 'gentil' or aristocratic nature of this couple (see pp. 13–14).

54 *That trewely ...*: note the tenses. 'She *has* the keeping of Chauntecleer's heart, fast found in every limb. He *loved* her so that his happiness was complete.'

But such a Ioye was it to here hem singe,
Whan that the brighte sonne gan to springe,
In swete accord, 'my lief is faren in londe.'
For thilke tyme, as I have understonde,   60
Bestes and briddes coude speke and singe.
   And so bifel, that in a daweninge,
As Chauntecleer among his wyves alle
Sat on his perche, that was in the halle,
And next him sat this faire Pertelote,
This Chauntecleer gan gronen in his throte,
As man that in his dreem is drecched sore.
And whan that Pertelote thus herde him rore,
She was agast, and seyde, 'O herte dere,
What eyleth yow, to grone in this manere?   70
Ye been a verray sleper, fy for shame!'
And he answerde and seyde thus, 'madame,
I pray yow, that ye take it nat a-grief:
By god, me mette I was in swich meschief
Right now, that yet myn herte is sore afright.
Now god,' quod he, 'my swevene recche aright,
And keep my body out of foul prisoun!
Me mette, how that I romed up and doun
Withinne our yerde, wher-as I saugh a beste,
Was lyk an hound, and wolde han maad areste   80
Upon my body, and wolde han had me deed
His colour was bitwixe yelwe and reed;
And tipped was his tail, and bothe his eres,
With blak, unlyk the remenant of his heres;
His snowte smal, with glowinge eyen tweye.
Yet of his look for fere almost I deye;
This caused me my groning, doutelees.'
   'Avoy!' quod she, 'fy on yow, hertelees!
Allas!' quod she, 'for, by that god above,
Now han ye lost myn herte and al my love;   90
I can nat love a coward, by my feith.
For certes, what so any womman seith,
We alle desyren, if it mighte be,
To han housbondes hardy, wyse, and free,
And secree, and no nigard, ne no fool,
Ne him that is agast of every tool,

59 *'my lief is faren in londe'*: this is an actual medieval song and contains the line: 'She hath my hert in hold'.

60 *For thilke tyme* . . .: for some background on beast fables, see Introduction, pp. 27–9 and 38–43.

67 *As man that* . . .: like a man that. The warm, comic identification of these two birds – this man and wife – is fully developed from now on and becomes the controlling impression of the poem here.

71 *Ye been a verray sleper* . . .: 'What a sound sleeper you are!' The tone is ironic and establishes Pertelote's character very strongly.

73 *take it nat a-grief*: don't be alarmed.

76 *recche aright*: interpret correctly, i.e. bring to a happy ending.

79 *a beste*: for an analysis of Russel the fox, see Introduction, pp. 76–9.

88 *'Avoy!'* . . .: 'Get away with you!' Pertelote rounds on her husband for his cowardice – something we still associate colloquially with 'chicken'. Her tone is wonderfully vivid and not at all what we associate with a fine lady. For a discussion of marriage and 'maistrie', see Introduction, pp. 55–68.

94 *hardy, wyse, and free* . . .: these were the conventional requirements of a good husband.

Ne noon avauntour, by that god above!
How dorste ye seyn for shame unto your love,
That any thing mighte make yow aferd?
Have ye no mannes herte, and han a berd?   100
Allas! and conne ye been agast of swevenis?
No-thing, god wot, but vanitee, in sweven is.
Swevenes engendren of replecciouns,
And ofte of fume, and of complecciouns,
Whan humours been to habundant in a wight.
Certes this dreem, which ye han met to-night,
Cometh of the grete superfluitee
Of youre rede *colera*, pardee,
Which causeth folk to dreden in here dremes
Of arwes, and of fyr with rede lemes,   110
Of grete bestes, that they wol hem byte,
Of contek, and of whelpes grete and lyte;
Right as the humour of malencolye
Causeth ful many a man, in sleep, to crye,
For fere of blake beres, or boles blake,
Or elles, blake develes wole hem take.
Of othere humours coude I telle also,
That werken many a man in sleep ful wo;
But I wol passe as lightly as I can.
    Lo Catoun, which that was so wys a man,   120
Seyde he nat thus, ne do no fors of dremes?
Now, sire,' quod she, 'whan we flee fro the bemes,
For Goddes love, as tak som laxatyf;
Up peril of my soule, and of my lyf,
I counseille yow the beste, I wol nat lye,
That bothe of colere and of malencolye
Ye purge yow; and for ye shul nat tarie,
Though in this toun is noon apotecarie,
I shal my-self to herbes techen yow,
That shul ben for your hele, and for your prow;   130
And in our yerd tho herbes shal I finde,
The whiche han of hir propretee, by kinde,
To purgen yow binethe, and eek above.
Forget not this, for goddes owene love!
Ye been ful colerik of compleccioun.
Ware the sonne in his ascencioun

100   *mannes herte ....:* a beautiful comic touch; though, if we follow the scholar who has identified Chauntecleer and Pertelote as Golden Spangled Hamburgs (see pp. 28 and 38), then it is to be remembered that this species does indeed have tufts that resemble beards.

102   *vanitee:* emptiness. For a discussion of dreams, see Introduction, pp. 60–68.

103   *replecciouns:* for a discussion of Pertelote's medical knowledge in the debate, see Introduction, pp. 61–3.

120   *Catoun:* Dionysius Cato, the author of *Disticha Catonis,* a collection of sayings in Latin verses (or distichs) which was a common school textbook. Pertelote translates its *somnia ne cures* correctly here. This citing of authorities (see Introduction, pp. 20 and 63–4) marks this section of the poem out as a mock scholarly dispute.

123   *as tak:* please take.

124   *Up peril:* upon peril.

132   *propretee:* 'which have naturally [*by kynde*], from their special power [*propretee*] ways to purge you by vomiting or excretion'.

135   *colerik of compleccioun:* predominantly choleric in your blending of humours.

136   *the sonne in his ascencioun:* beware, as a man of 'colerik' temperament, of becoming overheated as the sun reaches its zenith. Chickens are particularly sensitive to heat and pant in over-high temperatures. Compare ll. 448–9.

Ne fynde yow nat repleet of humours hote;
And if it do, I dar wel leye a grote,
That ye shul have a fevere terciane,
Or an agu, that may be youre bane.   140
A day or two ye shul have digestyves
Of wormes, er ye take your laxatyves,
Of lauriol, centaure, and fumetere,
Or elles of ellebor, that groweth there,
Of catapuce, or of gaytres beryis,
Or erbe yve, growing in our yerd, that mery is;
Pekke hem up right as they growe, and ete hem in.
Be mery, housbond, for your fader kin!
Dredeth no dreem; I can say yow na-more.'
     'Madame,' quod he, '*graunt mercy* of your lore.   150
But nathelees, as touching daun Catoun,
That hath of wisdom such a greet renoun,
Though that he bad no dremes for to drede,
By god, men may in olde bokes rede
Of many a man, more of auctoritee
Than ever Catoun was, so mote I thee,
That al the revers seyn of his sentence,
And han wel founden by experience,
That dremes ben significaciouns,
As wel of Ioye as tribulaciouns   160

141-2   *digestyves of wormes*: these are natural food for a hen but were also recommended by Dioscorides against tertian fevers in humans. Tertian fevers are those that increase in violence every other (*not* every third) day.

143   *lauriol*: spurge laurel (*Daphne laureola*), which *A Boke of the Properties of Herbes* (1550) states 'wyll make a man laxatyve and it is good to purge a man of flewme and of the coler'.

   centaure: centaury, a member of the gentian family whose properties are the same as those of the laurel.

   fumetere: fumitory, another purge for melancholy which 'openeth the lyver and ... clereth a man's blode'.

144   *ellebor*: there are two types of hellebore, black and white. The first 'purgeth the coleryke blacke humours', according to *The Great Herball of Treviris* (1526); the second, particularly effective against phlegm, 'purgeth upward by vomyte'.

145   *catapuce*: according to *The Great Herball of Treviris*, this is 'the frute or sede of a tree that is called catapucia'. Whatever this is, its fruit 'hath vertu to purge the flewmes principally, and secondly the melancholyke & coleryke humours. It hath might to purge above because it causeth wind that restrayneth the humoures upwarde.'

   gaytres beryis: buckthorn berries – a purgative.

146   *erbe yve*: perhaps the ground ivy which is said to alleviate indigestion, or buck's horn plantain, which was said to cure jaundice and tertian fevers. The point here is the accuracy and irony of this hen's knowledge of the plants that would indeed cure Chauntecleer had he the symptoms his wife detects. This enthusiastic pedantry is charmingly offset by the rhythm of l. 147.

148   *your fader kin*: compare ll. 482–91. Chauntecleer's pride in his ancestry is part of the larger discussion of this sin in the work as a whole; see Introduction, pp. 10, 30–32, 43–6 and 68–70.

150   *graunt mercy of your lore*: a formal phrase in a disputation that disposes of an inferior's argument by appealing to other authorities. Chauntecleer is about to launch into a lengthy monologue on dreams and dream lore which, while it shows him to be something of an authority himself, ends in his refusing to care for the validity of dreams at all. For a discussion of this, see Introduction, pp. 60–68. The whole is an example of Chaucer's comedy at its wisest and shrewdest.

156   *so mote I thee*: so may I prosper.

157   *That al the revers ...*: that hold exactly the opposite of his opinion.

That folk enduren in this lyf present.
Ther nedeth make of this noon argument:
The verray preve sheweth it in dede.
   Oon of the gretteste auctours that men rede
Seith thus, that whylom two felawes wente
On pilgrimage, in a ful good entente;
And happed so, thay come into a toun,
Wher-as ther was swich congregacioun
Of peple, and eek so streit of herbergage,
That they ne founde as muche as o cotage,   170
In which they bothe mighte y-logged be.
Wherfor thay mosten, of necessitee,
As for that night, departen compaignye;
And ech of hem goth to his hostelrye,
And took his logging as it wolde falle.
That oon of hem was logged in a stalle,
Fer in a yerd, with oxen of the plough;
That other man was logged wel y-nough,
As was his aventure, or his fortune,
That us governeth alle as in commune.   180
   And so bifel, that, longe er it were day,
This man mette in his bed, ther-as he lay,
How that his felawe gan up-on him calle,
And seyde, 'allas! for in an oxes stalle
This night I shal be mordred ther I lye.
Now help me, dere brother, er I dye;
In alle haste com to me,' he sayde.
This man out of his sleep for fere abrayde;
But whan that he was wakned of his sleep,
He turned him, and took of this no keep;   190
Him thoughte his dreem nas but a vanitee.
Thus twyës in his sleping dremed he.
And atte thridde tyme yet his felawe
Cam, as him thoughte, and seide, 'I am now slawe;
Bihold my blody woundes, depe and wyde!
Arys up erly in the morwe-tyde,
And at the west gate of the toun,' quod he,
'A carte ful of donge ther shaltow see,
In which my body is hid ful prively;
Do thilke carte aresten boldely.   200

163 *The verray prevè*: experience shows it in practice. A deeply ironic comment!

164 *Oon of the gretteste ...*: analogous tales to that which follows are found in classical sources – e.g. Cicero's *De divinatione* – but research has shown that Chaucer possibly derived it from a contemporary source, the *Super sapientiam Salomonis* of Robert Holkot. For the significance of this, see Introduction, pp. 20, 45–6 and 60–68. Of course, Chauntecleer's telling a story of dream prophecies heeded too late is ironic when we consider what happens to him. This is a further aspect of Chaucer's kindly but serious irony concerning man's pride in his intellectual abilities.

169 *streit of herbergage*: short on accommodation.

179 *aventure, or his fortune*: chance or luck. This is an early mention of the theme of chance and predestination which is of the greatest importance to the story. For a discussion, see Introduction, pp. 33 and 46–50, and notes to ll. 413ff.

197 *west gate*: the gate on the west side of a walled medieval town. In many cases the gates gave their name to that part of the town around them, a name that often cases (e.g. Oxford) still survives.

200 *Do thilke carte aresten*: have that cart stopped.

My gold caused my mordre, sooth to sayn;'
And tolde him every poynt how he was slayn,
With a ful pitous face, pale of hewe.
And truste wel, his dreem he fond ful trewe;
For on the morwe, as sone as it was day,
To his felawes in he took the way;
And whan that he cam to this oxes stalle,
After his felawe he bigan to calle.

   The hostiler answered him anon,
And seyde, 'sire, your felawe is agon,   210
As sone as day he wente out of the toun.'
This man gan fallen in suspecioun,
Remembring on his dremes that he mette,
And forth he goth, no lenger wolde he lette,
Unto the west gate of the toun, and fond
A dong-carte, as it were to donge lond,
That was arrayed in the same wyse
As ye han herd the dede man devyse;
And with an hardy herte he gan to crye
Vengeaunce and Iustice of this felonye: –   220
'My felawe mordred is this same night,
And in this carte he lyth gapinge upright.
I crye out on the ministres,' quod he,
'That sholden kepe and reulen this citee;
Harrow! allas! her lyth my felawe slayn!'
What sholde I more un-to this tale sayn?
The peple out-sterte, and caste the cart to grounde,
And in the middel of the dong they founde
The dede man, that mordred was al newe.

   O blisful god, that art so Iust and trewe!   230
Lo, how that thou biwreyest mordre alway!
Mordre wol out, that see we day by day.
Mordre is so wlatsom and abhominable
To god, that is so Iust and resonable,
That he ne wol nat suffre it heled be;
Though it abyde a yeer, or two, or three,
Mordre wol out, this my conclusioun.
And right anoon, ministres of that toun
Han hent the carter, and so sore him pyned,
And eek the hostiler so sore engyned,   240

210   *agon*: departed, with the sense of left and died.

212   *gan fallen in suspecioun*: became suspicious.

216   *as it were*: as it seemed.

222   *gapinge upright*: a vivid phrase to be translated 'face up with his mouth open'.

226   *What sholde I*: why should I?

227   *out-sterte*: rushed out.

230   *O blisful god*: at the head of this paragraph in one of the best manuscripts of the poem the word *auctor* is written in the margin. We have seen (Introduction, pp. 83–94) that Chaucer or another would have read the poem aloud. This suggests that the audience would have had the passage read to them in such a tone as to make to clear that this was Chaucer speaking in his own voice.

233   *abhominable*: Chaucer seems to have derived the word from *ab homine*: 'against the nature of man'. The correct etymology is from *abominari*: 'turn away from evil omens'.

239–40   *pyned ... engyned*: such judicial cruelty is somewhat more elaborately described in *The Prioress's Tale*. This, along with the reference to St Kenelm in both stories, may suggest some implicit criticism of the Prioress by her priest; see Introduction, p. 85.

That thay biknewe hir wikkednesse anoon,
And were an-hanged by the nekke-boon.
  Here may men seen that dremes been to drede.
And certes, in the same book I rede,
Right in the nexte chapitre after this,
(I gabbe nat, so have I Ioye or blis,)
Two men that wolde han passed over see,
For certeyn cause, in-to a fer contree,
If that the wind ne hadde been contrarie,
That made hem in a citee for to tarie,   250
That stood ful mery upon an haven-syde.
But on a day, agayn the even-tyde,
The wind gan chaunge, and blew right as hem leste.
Iolif and glad they wente un-to hir reste,
And casten hem ful erly for to saille;
But to that oo man fil a greet mervaille.
That oon of hem, in sleping as he lay,
Him mette a wonder dreem, agayn the day;
Him thoughte a man stood by his beddes syde,
And him comaunded, that he sholde abyde,   260
And seyde him thus, 'if thou to-morwe wende,
Thou shalt be dreynt; my tale is at an ende.'
He wook, and tolde his felawe what he mette.
And preyde him his viage for to lette;
As for that day, he preyde him to abyde.
His felawe, that lay by his beddes syde,
Gan for to laughe, and scorned him ful faste.
'No dreem,' quod he, 'may so myn herte agaste,
That I wol lette for to do my thinges.
I sette not a straw by thy dreminges,   270
For swevenes been but vanitees and Iapes.
Men dreme al-day of owles or of apes,
And eke of many a mase therwithal;
Men dreme of thing that nevere was ne shal.
But sith I see that thou wolt heer abyde,
And thus for-sleuthen wilfully thy tyde,
Got wot it reweth me; and have good day.'
And thus he took his leve, and wente his way.
But er that he hadde halfe his cours y-seyled,
Noot I nat why, ne what mischaunce it eyled,   280

245   *the nexte chapitre*: the story of the shipwreck appears next to the preceding tale in none of the known sources. The effect is probably designed to suggest Chauntecleer's enthusiasm. This it does most successfully.

249–51   *that the wind ... haven-syde*: the syntax is confused by the repetition of 'that' but the sequence of ideas is clear enough.

252   *agayn the even-tyde*: towards evening.

258   *agayn the day*: towards morning. Dreams after midnight were considered particularly auspicious (see pp. 65–6).

267   *scorned him ful faste*: poured scorn on him.

268–9   *'No dreem ... do my thinges*: no dream will frighten me so much that it will prevent me from attending to my business affairs.

272   *of owles or of apes*: this is a famous and much discussed phrase. It relates to the whole question of animal symbolism which is discussed in the Introduction, pp. 38–43. The background seems to be as follows. The owl is an iconographic representation of the Jews, its love of darkness being a 'type' or representation of the Jews' rejection of the teaching of Christ. Filthy habits were associated with it and it came to be regarded further as a type of unclean sensuality. In the Bestiaries (see Introduction, pp. 41–2), the ape is seen as an evil animal associated with the Fall and with Satan. The animals were quite frequently paired in medieval art and what the man who will drown scoffs at is dream symbols of evil.

273   *mase*: a delusion; but perhaps, in a more specific sense, a reference to the mazes found on the pavements of some medieval cathedrals (e.g. Chartres) which symbolize the soul's pilgrimage through the wilderness of the world and its inevitable end. Again, the sceptic refuses the warnings implicit in symbolism.

But casuelly the shippes botme rente,
And ship and man under the water wente
In sighte of othere shippes it byside,
That with hem seyled at the same tyde.
And therfor, faire Pertelote so dere,
By swiche ensamples olde maistow lere,
That no man sholde been to recchelees
Of dremes, for I sey thee, doutelees,
That many a dreem ful sore is for to drede.
   Lo, in the lyf of seint Kenelm, I rede,   290
That was Kenulphus sone, the noble king
Of Mercenrike, how Kenelm mette a thing;
A lyte er he was mordred, on a day,
His mordre in his avisioun he say.
His norice him expouned every del
His sweven, and bad him for to kepe him wel
For traisoun; but he nas but seven yeer old,
And therfore litel tale hath he told
Of any dreem, so holy was his herte.
By god, I hadde lever than my sherte   300
That ye had rad his legende, as have I.
Dame Pertelote, I sey yow trewely,
Macrobeus, that writ the avisioun
In Affrike of the worthy Cipioun,
Affermeth dremes, and seith that they been
Warning of thinges that men after seen.
   And forther-more, I pray yow loketh wel
In the olde testament, of Daniel,
If he held dremes any vanitee.
Reed eek of Ioseph, and ther shul ye see   310
Wher dremes ben somtyme (I sey nat alle)
Warning of thinges that shul after falle.
Loke of Egipt the king, daun Pharao,
His bakere and his boteler also,
Wher they ne felte noon effect in dremes.
Who-so wol seken actes of sondry remes,
May rede of dremes many a wonder thing.
   Lo Cresus, which that was of Lyde king,
Mette he nat that he sat upon a tree,
Which signified he sholde anhanged be?   320

281   *casuelly*: by some mischance. The lack of an adequate explanation makes the sense of warning stronger.

286   *ensamples olde*: the medieval use of authorities to illustrate ideas is discussed in the Introduction, pp. 20 and 63–4.

290   *lyf of seint Kenelm*: lives of saints and other religious people in prose or verse were popular in the middle ages. *The Prioress's Tale* is one such telling of the martyrdom of the boy saint Hugh of Lincoln. The Nun's Priest's use of the legend of St Kenelm may be seen as an ironic comment on this (see Introduction, p. 85). St Kenelm was also a boy martyr. He succeeded to the throne of Mercia in England in 821 at the age of seven. His ambitious sister schemed to have him murdered. He had a dream of climbing a tree which was then cut down, releasing his soul to fly away. His nurse interpreted the dream as a portent, but the boy was too young and innocent to take any notice. The legend is apocryphal.

298   *litel tale hath he told*: he attached little importance.

300   *I hadde lever than my sherte* ...: 'I would give my shirt for you to have been able to read this legend as I have.' A marvellously humorous image.

303   *Macrobeus* ...: Macrobius Theodosius (c. AD 400) wrote a commentary on Cicero's *De Republica* which includes quotations from the sixth book, in which Scipio relates a dream in which his grandfather (known as Scipio Africanus Major) appeared to him and, leading him to the Milky Way, showed him that he would conquer Carthage. In his commentary, Macrobius discusses the various types of dreams men may have and so became an authority on dreams for the whole middle ages. The book was well known to Chaucer.

308   *In the olde testament* ...: Chauntecleer turns to cite Old Testament authorities in the conventional manner of medieval sermon and debate. The prophet Daniel is shown to have interpreted several dreams. Joseph read the dreams of the Egyptian Pharaoh and of his butler and baker, so warning the country against starvation and thereby promoting his own career.

318   *Lo Cresus* ...: Chauntecleer turns to classical authorities and quotes the story that formed the last of the Monk's recitals, see pp. 96–9.

Lo heer Andromacha, Ectores wyf,
That day that Ector sholde lese his lyf,
She dremed on the same night biforn,
How that the lyf of Ector sholde be lorn,
If thilke day he wente in-to bataille;
She warned him, but it mighte nat availle;
He wente for to fighte nathelees,
But he was slayn anoon of Achilles.
But thilke tale is al to long to telle,
And eek it is ny day, I may nat dwelle.   330
Shortly I seye, as for conclusioun,
That I shal han of this avisioun
Adversitee; and I seye forther-more,
That I ne telle of laxatyves no store,
For they ben venimous, I woot it wel;
I hem defye, I love hem never a del.

 Now let us speke of mirthe, and stinte al this;
Madame Pertelote, so have I blis,
Of o thing god hath sent me large grace;
For whan I see the beautee of your face,   340

321 *Andromacha*: Homer does not record Andromache having such a dream, but the middle ages made the story of Troy their own, adding to it such incidents as this and the story of Troilus and Criseyde which Chaucer made into his greatest completed narrative. The dream of Andromache would have been familiar from these retellings.

331 *I may nat dwelle*: Chauntecleer must not neglect to crow at daybreak.

334 *telle of laxatyves*: Chauntecleer reaffirms his faith in his dream and (very humanly) refuses the laxatives on the grounds that they are unpleasant. After all his display of learning we suddenly see him in very natural terms again. This prepares us for the next paragraph.

Ye ben so scarlet-reed about your yĕn,
It maketh al my drede for to dyen;
For, also siker as *In principio*,
Mulier est hominis confusio;
Madame, the sentence of this Latin is –
Womman is mannes Ioye and al his blis.
For whan I fele a-night your softe syde,
Al-be-it that I may nat on you ryde,
For that our perche is maad so narwe, alas!
I am so ful of Ioye and of solas   350
That I defye bothe sweven and dreem.'
And with that word he fley doun fro the beem,
For it was day, and eek his hennes alle;
And with a chuk he gan hem for to calle,
For he had founde a corn, lay in the yerd.
Royal he was, he was namore aferd;

341   *Ye ben so scarlet-reed* ...: such a colour is the sign of a laying hen. The expression of physical desire is delightful and ironic (white faces were most admired for beauty in the middle ages) but it also suggests in a very comprehensible way the stirring of the love for his wife that clouds Chauntecleer's intellect. This theme takes us to the heart of the poem and is discussed in the Introduction on pp. 44–5 and 55–70.

343   *In principio* ...: Chauntecleer's confused scholarship is here of the greatest importance, see Introduction, pp. 44–5, 57–9, 66–7 and 87–90. The would-be authority on dreams has just expressed his love for his wife. Now he erroneously tries to prove from learned sources that marital bliss is the highest good.

In principio. This is the opening of St John's Gospel: 'In the beginning was the word.' This was the most popular gospel excerpt of the middle ages. *In principio* became the name of the first fourteen verses of St John which were synonymous with absolute biblical truth. Chauntecleer claims that what he says next is just as true as these.

What in fact he says – *mulier est hominis confusio* – means 'woman is man's confusion or ruin'. Chauntecleer translates the phrase to mean just the opposite. Far from being man's ruin, Chauntecleer, swept away by love of his wife, declares that woman is man's 'Ioye and al his blis'. He has forgotten that, in the beginning, Adam, overcome by love of Eve, ate the apple from the tree of knowledge which she had already tasted and so was expelled from Paradise with her. Thus, right at the start of human history, woman led to man's destruction. In biblical terms, the phrase *mulier est hominis confusio* is absolutely true.

Chauntecleer repeats Adam's sin. He puts love of his wife before what he knows to be true. Her charms make him forget the warnings in his dream. Overcome by female charm in this way, he struts to his confusion. However, we should also be aware of the ambiguity here. In many respects Chauntecleer's mistranslation conveys a profoundly human truth. For a discussion of this and the significance of Chauntecleer's repetition of Adam's sin, the clouding of his mind so that he forgets his dream warnings and the relation of this to the issues of free will and salvation which are about to be mentioned in the poem, see the references above.

348   *I may nat on you ryde*: a poignant touch which at once emphasizes Chauntecleer's sexual desire for his wife (which we know to be excessive) and makes us sympathetic towards it.

352   *fley*: flew.

355   *a corn, lay in the yerd*: a grain of wheat that lay in the yard.

356   *Royal he was* ...: for a discussion of Chauntecleer as a prince, see pp. 9–10 and 54–5.

He fethered Pertelote twenty tyme,
And trad as ofte, er that it was pryme.
He loketh as it were a grim leoun;
And on his toos he rometh up and doun,   360
Him deyned not to sette his foot to grounde.
He chukketh, whan he hath a corn y-founde,
And to him rennen thanne his wyves alle.
Thus royal, as a prince is in his halle,
Leve I this Chauntecleer in his pasture;
And after wol I telle his aventure.

    Whan that the month in which the world bigan,
That highte March, whan god first maked man,
Was complet, and y-passed were also,
Sin March bigan, thritty dayes and two,   370
Bifel that Chauntecleer, in al his pryde,
His seven wyves walking by his syde,
Caste up his eyen to the brighte sonne,
That in the signe of Taurus hadde y-ronne
Twenty degrees and oon, and somwhat more;
And knew by kynde, and by noon other lore,
That it was pryme, and crew with blisful stevene.
'The sonne,' he sayde, 'is clomben up on hevene
Fourty degrees and oon, and more, y-wis.
Madame Pertelote, my worldes blis,   380

357   *He fethered Pertelote* ...: a vivid revelation of his sexual love! But for a discussion of what was held to be the true place of sexuality in marriage, see pp. 55–60.

358   *pryme*: the period from 6 to 9 a.m.

359   *leoun*: lions are conventional symbols of pride and were frequently associated with this, the chief of the Seven Deadly Sins (see Introduction, pp. 43–6, 68–70 and 87–90). We should also note that Pliny among the ancient historians believed that the proud bearing of a cock would overawe a lion.

360   *on his toos*: this is exactly the proud, ridiculous strutting of a cockerel.

367   *Whan that the month* ...: this intricate passage – partly a satire on over-complex ways of calculation adopted at the period – is not wholly clear. The date Chaucer is trying to suggest is probably 3 May.

Early theologians (among them Bede and St Ambrose) assumed that the creation took place on or about 21 March, the day of the vernal equinox. This accounts for the first line of the paragraph. Assuming (and this is disputed) that ll. 369–70 mean 'when March was complete and thirty-two days had also passed' we arrive at 3 May. The obvious problem here is the phrase 'sin March began', which is probably a verbal confusion best omitted. Further, we are told in ll. 374–5 that the sun had gone a little over 21° into Taurus. This gives us a date of 2 May, 'and somwhat more' – in other words 3 May. To arrive at this configuration we must recall that the sun was supposed to enter the zodiac sign of Taurus on 11 April. As each day corresponds to one degree of the circle of the zodiac, eleven days of March, plus the thirty days or degrees of Aries plus the twenty-one of Taurus, gives us a date of 2 May. However, when we take into account the 'somwhat more', the date calculated by the zodiac gives us the same date as that calculated by the months, namely 3 May.

376   *by kynde*: by instinct. Chauntecleer knows the time by instinct, but the astronomical lore he brings in to support his case allows us to fix the date as 3 May again. The daily altitude of the sun determines the hour of the day. On 3 May the sun would have risen a little over 41° by the close of *pryme* – i.e. 9 a.m.

Herkneth thise blisful briddes how they singe,
And see the fresshe floures how they springe;
Ful is myn herte of revel and solas.'
But sodeinly him fil a sorweful cas;
For ever the latter ende of Ioye is wo.
God woot that worldly Ioye is sone ago;
And if a rethor coude faire endyte,
He in a cronique saufly mighte it wryte,
As for a sovereyn notabilitee.
Now every wys man, lat him herkne me;   390
This storie is al-so trewe, I undertake,
As is the book of Launcelot de Lake,
That wommen holde in ful gret reverence.
Now wol l torne agayn to my sentence.
    A col-fox, ful of sly iniquitee,
That in the grove hadde woned yeres three,
By heigh imaginacioun forn-cast,
The same night thurgh-out the hegges brast
Into the yerd, ther Chauntecleer the faire
Was wont, and eek his wyves, to repaire;   400
And in a bed of wortes stille he lay,
Til it was passed undern of the day,
Wayting his tyme on Chauntecleer to falle,
As gladly doon thise homicydes alle,
That in awayt liggen to mordre men.
O false mordrer, lurking in thy den!
O newe Scariot, newe Genilon!
False dissimilour, O Greek Sinon,
That broghtest Troye al outrely to sorwe!
O Chauntecleer, acursed be that morwe,   410
That thou into that yerd flough fro the bemes!
Thou were ful wel y-warned by thy dremes,
That thilke day was perilous to thee.
But what that god forwoot mot nedes be,
After the opinioun of certeyn clerkis.
Witnesse on him, that any perfit clerk is,
That in scole is gret altercacioun
In this matere, and greet disputisoun,
And hath ben of an hundred thousand men.
But I ne can not bulte it to the bren,   420

381 *thise blisful briddes*: a delightful display of pride just before this bird's fall.

387 *a rethor...*: a rhetorician. Chauntecleer's adventure should be written up so that it can stand for all time as an example of sudden reverses in fortune. The idea, needless to say, is ironic; while the tone is a satire on high-flown rhetoric (compare ll. 406–11 and 518–34). This criticism of poetic style is an important part of Chaucer's purpose and effect; see pp. 90–91.

392 *Launcelot de Lake*: an Arthurian hero and the lover of Arthur's queen Guinivere. The Nun's Priest says his story is as true as this – in other words it is a complete fabrication suitable for women who avidly believe such tales. Chaucer, of course, antedates Malory and whatever version of the Lancelot story he is referring to was almost certainly in French. This would have caused no problems in a bilingual court. For a fuller discussion, see pp. 11–12 and 91–2.

395 *col-fox*: the phrase has caused much debate. It suggests Russel's black markings.

397 *heigh imaginacioun forn-cast*: this may mean either 'foreseen by the exalted imagination' and so refers to Chauntecleer's dream; or 'pre-destined by God' and so is a foretaste of the discussion on free will that is to ensue.

402 *undern*: the stretch of time between 9 a.m. and noon.

407–8 *Scariot ... Genilon ... Sinon*: Judas Iscariot betrayed Christ; Ganelon, the traitor in the great early French epic the *Chanson de Roland*, betrayed the rearguard of Charlemagne's army; Sinon was the traitor who persuaded the inhabitants of Troy to let in the wooden horse. This passage of ironic rhetoric thus brings together traitors from three great areas of medieval literature. The effect is deliberately and absurdly disproportionate to the subject here.

414 *what that god forwoot ...*: that which God has foreknowledge of. The issue of God's foreknowledge and the degree to which man is responsible for his actions and so for his salvation was of the greatest importance to many people of the time and not just those in academic circles. Chaucer knew there was 'gret altercacioun' about the issue. He was deeply concerned in it, but his discussion in *The Nun's Priest's Tale*, far from being intended to settle the issue, airs the various current views while casting a distinctly ironic glance at man's intellectual pretensions. For a more detailed discussion, see pp. 46–50.

420 *bulte it to the bren*: 'sift the flour [what is valuable] from the bran [that which is worthless]'. Compare l. 623.

As can the holy doctour Augustyn,
Or Boece, or the bishop Bradwardyn,
Whether that goddes worthy forwiting
Strey neth me nedely for to doon a thing,
(Nedely clepe I simple necessitee);
Or elles, if free choys be graunted me
To do that same thing, or do it noght,
Though god forwoot it, er that it was wroght;
Or if his witing streyneth nevere a del
But by necessitee condicionel.   430
I wol not han to do of swich matere;
My tale is of a cok, as ye may here,
That took his counseil of his wyf, with sorwe,
To walken in the yerd upon that morwe
That he had met the dreem, that I yow tolde.
Wommennes counseils been ful ofte colde;
Wommannes counseil broghte us first to wo,
And made Adam fro paradys to go,
Ther-as he was ful mery, and wel at ese.
But for I noot, to whom it mighte displese,   440
If I counseil of wommen wolde blame,
Passe over, for I seyde it in my game.
Rede auctours, wher they trete of swich matere,
And what thay seyn of wommen ye may here.

421 *Augustyn*: St Augustine of Hippo (354–430); see pp. 49–50.

422 *Boece*: Boethius (d. 524), author of *The Consolation of Philosophy*, one of Chaucer's favourite books and a text which he translated. See pp. 15 and 50.

Bradwardyn: Thomas Bradwardine (d. 1349), Archbishop of Canterbury and a leading figure in the contemporary debate over free will. For the ideas of all three men, see pp. 49–50.

423 *goddes worthy forwiting*: the passage brings together ideas on free will from Boethius but relates also to Augustine and Bradwardine. There are three propositions put forward here:

(i) God knows and ordains all that happens and so man's actions are predestined, ll. 423–5. This is 'simple necessitee'.

(ii) God knows all that happens but leaves man free to take the decisions he knows he will take, ll. 426–8.

(iii) God knows all that happens and ordains some events but leaves men free in others to take the decisions he knows he will take, ll. 429–30. The relative degree of freedom in the second part of this description is 'necessitee condicionel'.

The underlying gist is this: man does not know if his actions are wholly under God's control, wholly in his own control, or partly one and partly the other. In all cases God knows what will happen. The Nun's Priest, having outlined the dilemma, wisely declares he will have nothing to do with it. 'My tale is of a cok,' he says. For the implications of this, see pp. 50 and 92.

433 *took his counseil of his wyf*: Chauntecleer, as we have seen, repeats Adam's sin of uxoriousness and so exemplifies original sin. The following lines make the analogy clear.

436 *colde*: baneful, harmful. This was a standard opinion, but the speaker is not happy with it and claims he is not in earnest. He wants to pass over the subject lest he offend some people. He recommends we read the authorities on the subject.

Thise been the cokkes wordes, and nat myne;
I can noon harm of no womman divyne.

    Faire in the sond, to bathe hir merily,
Lyth Pertelote, and alle hir sustres by,
Agayn the sonne; and Chauntecleer so free
Song merier than the mermayde in the see;   450
For Phisiologus seith sikerly,
How that they singen wel and merily.
And so bifel that, as he caste his yë,
Among the wortes, on a boterflye,
He was war of this fox that lay ful lowe.
No-thing ne liste him thanne for to crowe,
But cryde anon, 'cok, cok,' and up he sterte,
As man that was affrayed in his herte.
For naturelly a beest desyreth flee
Fro his contrarie, if he may it see,   460
Though he never erst had seyn it with his yë.

    This Chauntecleer, whan he gan him espye,
He wolde han fled, but that the fox anon
Seyde, 'Gentil sire, allas! wher wol ye gon?
Be ye affrayed of me that am your freend?
Now certes, I were worse than a feend,
If I to yow wolde harm or vileinye.
I am nat come your counseil for tespye;
But trewely, the cause of my cominge
Was only for to herkne how that ye singe.   470
For trewely ye have as mery a stevene
As eny aungel hath, that is in hevene;
Therwith ye han in musik more felinge
Than hadde Boece, or any that can singe.
My lord your fader (god his soule blesse!)
And eek your moder, of hir gentilesse,
Han in myn hous y-been, to my gret ese;
And certes, sire, ful fayn wolde I yow plese.
But for men speke of singing, I wol saye,
So mote I brouke wel myn eyen tweye,   480
Save yow, I herde never man so singe,
As dide your fader in the morweninge;
Certes, it was of herte, al that he song.
And for to make his voys the more strong,

445 *Thise been the cokkes wordes* ...: the desire to disclaim responsibility for speaking harshly about women is clear. What the poet has in fact done by this seeming *non sequitur* is first to undermine the misogynistic element in the biblical parallel of Chauntecleer and Pertelote to Adam and Eve; prepare us in this way – if we choose to think that it is the Nun's Priest talking – for the revelation of his personality in the later lines; and finally to break the dramatic coherence of this long paragraph. After all the high-falutin rhetoric, philosophy and religious dogmatism we return happily to the farmyard and Pertelote in her dustbath.

450 *merier than the mermayde*: Chaucer tells us in the next line that he derived the mermaid from *Physiologus*, a work probably from second-century Alexandria, in which animals both natural and imaginary are described in a way that reflects on human life. The mermaid, for example, has a merry song because it is like the pleasures of the world. It suggests bodily delights which the true Christian will overcome. We know that Chauntecleer is in the grip of these (see especially ll. 522–5) and Chaucer's reference to the *Physiologus* here allows us to see Chauntecleer the songster strutting towards the fox – who is the devil and catches those who live by the flesh. For a more detailed account of such matters, see pp. 38–43, 68–70 and 76–9.

459 *a beest desyreth flee* ...: a reference to the idea that every creature had an opposite to which it felt natural antipathy.

466 *I were worse than a feend*: as a symbol of the devil he is, of course.

474 *Boece*: Boethius who, in addition to handing to the early middle ages something of the traditions of ancient philosophy, also wrote an influential work on music.

480 *So mote I brouke wel myn eyen tweye*: 'So may I have good use of my two eyes!' A colloquial expression and somewhat ironic in view of his persuading Chauntecleer to close his eyes while singing, an idea first broached in ll. 486–7.

482 *fader*: the theme of family pride is an important aspect of the discussion of this Deadly Sin. Compare ll. 148 and 497–501, and see pp. 9–10 and 68–70.

He wolde so peyne him, that with bothe his yën
He moste winke, so loude he wolde cryen.
And stonden on his tiptoon ther-with-al,
And strecche forth his nekke long and smal.
And eek he was of swich discrecioun,
That ther nas no man in no regioun   490
That him in song or wisdom mighte passe.
I have wel rad in daun Burnel the Asse,
Among his vers, how that ther was a cok,
For that a preestes sone yaf him a knok
Upon his leg, whyl he was yong and nyce,
He made him for to lese his benefyce.
But certeyn, ther nis no comparisoun
Bitwix the wisdom and discrecioun
Of youre fader, and of his subtiltee.
Now singeth, sire, for seinte charitee,   500
Let see, conne ye your fader countrefete?'
This Chauntecleer his winges gan to bete,
As man that coude his tresoun nat espye,
So was he ravisshed with his flaterye.

   Allas! ye lordes, many a fals flatour
Is in your courtes, and many a losengeour,
That plesen yow wel more, by my feith,
Than he that soothfastnesse unto yow seith.
Redeth Ecclesiaste of flaterye;
Beth war, ye lordes, of hir trecherye.   510
   This Chauntecleer stood hye up-on his toos,
Strecching his nekke, and heeld his eyen cloos,
And gan to crowe loude for the nones;
And daun Russel the fox sterte up at ones,
And by the gargat hente Chauntecleer,
And on his bak toward the wode him beer,
For yet ne was ther no man that him sewed.
O destinee, that mayst nat been eschewed!
Allas, that Chauntecleer fleigh fro the bemes!
Allas, his wyf ne roghte nat of dremes!   520

492   *daun Burnel the Asse*: this animal fable is taken from *Speculum stultorum* or 'Mirror of Fools', a late-twelfth-century Latin satirical poem by Nigel Wireker, a monk of Christ Church, Canterbury. This particular episode tells how Gundulf, a priest's son, was one day chasing chickens from the yard with a stick and broke one of the chicken's legs in his enthusiasm. The chicken nursed its grievance for five years and, on the morning when Gundulf was to be ordained so that he might succeed to his father's benefice, refused to crow. Gundulf rose late, missed his ordination, and was ruined for life.

504   *So was he ravisshed . . .*: notice how Chaucer appears to 'freeze' this image by having a short paragraph of homily on the subject of flattery (derived from Ecclesiasties or Proverbs) before returning to the action and the very physical description of the 'ravisshed' Chauntecleer stretching out his neck to his would-be executioner. For a discussion of the ambiguous use of 'ravisshed', see p. 79.

515   *gargat*: throat. The bluntly physical tone is appropriate, but it is worth recalling that the sign of Taurus (l. 374) was associated with the head, neck and shoulders.

518   *O destinee . . .*: the tone from here to l. 554 is wryly satirical. A parody of high rhetoric is applied to a common farmyard catastrophe.

And on a Friday fil al this meschaunce.
O Venus, that art goddesse of plesaunce,
Sin that thy servant was this Chauntecleer,
And in thy service dide al his poweer,
More for delyt, than world to multiplye,
Why woldestow suffre him on thy day to dye?
O Gaufred, dere mayster soverayn,
That, whan thy worthy king Richard was slayn
With shot, compleynedest his deth so sore,
Why ne hadde I now thy sentence and thy lore,   530
The Friday for to chide, as diden ye?
(For on a Friday soothly slayn was he.)
Than wolde I shewe yow how that I coude pleyne
For Chauntecleres drede, and for his peyne.

    Certes, swich cry ne lamentacioun
Was never of ladies maad, whan Ilioun
Was wonne, and Pirrus with his streite swerd,
Whan he hadde hent king Priam by the berd,
And slayn him (as saith us *Eneydos*),
As maden alle the hennes in the clos,   540
Whan they had seyn of Chauntecleer the sighte.
But sovereynly dame Pertelote shrighte,
Ful louder than dide Hasdrubales wyf,
Whan that hir housbond hadde lost his lyf,
And that the Romayns hadde brend Cartage;
She was so ful of torment and of rage,
That wilfully into the fyr she sterte,
And brende hir-selven with a stedfast herte.
O woful hennes, right so cryden ye,
As, whan that Nero brende the citee   550
Of Rome, cryden senatoures wyves,
For that hir housbondes losten alle hir lyves;
Withouten gilt this Nero hath hem slayn.
Now wol I torne to my tale agayn.

    This sely widwe, and eek hir doghtres two,
Herden thise hennes crye and maken wo,
And out at dores sterten they anoon,
And syen the fox toward the grove goon,
And bar upon his bak the cok away;
And cryden, 'Out! harrow! and weylaway!   560

136

521 *Friday*: a traditionally unlucky day because of its association with the crucifixion. It is also the day associated with Venus (who has a strong astrological connection with Taurus). The goddess is evoked in the next lines. Chauntecleer is seen as her servant. He has given himself over to worldly love and the form of his sexuality is not that approved by the church. The worldly forces to which he has surrendered have no power to save him, and the apostrophe to Venus here is ironic (see Introduction, pp. 93–4).

527 *Gaufred*: the medieval rhetorician Geoffrey de Vinsauf whose Lament for Richard I is parodied here. For a discussion, see pp. 93–4. Notice that the phrase 'dere mayster soverayn' is ironic while the repetition of 'Friday' is absurdly banal.

536 *Ilioun*: Troy. As Chaucer tells us in l. 539 he has taken his description of the wailing women from Virgil's *Aeneid*, in which the slaying of Priam by Pyrrhus is recounted. This barnyard catastrophe is hardly the equivalent of the destruction of Troy but the comic effect is excellent. Notice also how the following references to Carthage and Rome allow Chaucer (elaborating on Geoffrey) to bring in the three great cities of the Latin world.

543 *Hasdrubales wyf*: Hasdrubal here was the leader of Carthage when it was sacked by Scipio Africanus Minor (for whom see note to l. 303) in 146 BC. Hasdrubal surrendered and his indignant wife threw herself and her children into the flames. Chaucer found the story in a work of St Jerome's which discusses the respective merits of widows, wives and virgins. It is also mentioned by Geoffrey.

546 *She was so ful ...*: Hasdrubal's wife, not Pertelote.

550 *Nero*: this famous incident is also mentioned by the Monk.

554 *Now wol I torne*: a wonderful example of Chaucer's comic skill and an effect that would have been enhanced by a public reading.

555 *This sely widwe ...*: this is a wonderfully vivid paragraph, full of real noise and gusto. The vigorous physical action is also just the release we need. Its direct appeal, however, should not blind us to the more serious suggestions which are discussed in the Introduction, pp. 80–87.

Ha, ha, the fox!' and after him they ran,
And eek with staves many another man;
Ran Colle our dogge, and Talbot, and Gerland,
And Malkin, with a distaf in hir hand;
Ran cow and calf, and eek the verray hogges
So were they fered for berking of the dogges
And shouting of the men and wimmen eke,
They ronne so, hem thoughte hir herte breke.
They yelleden as feendes doon in helle;
The dokes cryden as men wolde hem quelle;   570
The gees for fere flowen over the trees;
Out of the hyve cam the swarm of bees;
So hidous was the noyse, a! *benedicite!*
Certes, he Iakke Straw, and his meynee,
Ne made never shoutes half so shrille,
Whan that they wolden any Fleming kille,
As thilke day was maad upon the fox.
Of bras thay broghten bemes, and of box,
Of horn, of boon, in whiche they blewe and pouped,
And therwithal thay shryked and they houped;   580
It semed as that heven sholde falle.
Now, gode men, I pray yow herkneth alle!
    Lo, how fortune turneth sodeinly
The hope and pryde eek of hir enemy!
This cok, that lay upon the foxes bak,
In al his drede, un-to the fox he spak,
And seyde, 'sire, if that I were as ye,
Yet sholde I seyn (as wis god helpe me),
Turneth agayn, ye proude cherles alle!
A verray pestilence up-on yow falle!   590
Now am I come un-to this wodes syde,
Maugree your heed, the cock shal heer abyde;
I wol him ete in feith, and that anon.' –
The fox answerde, 'in feith, it shal be don,' –
And as he spak that word, al sodeinly
This cok brak from his mouth deliverly,
And heighe up-on a tree he fleigh anon.
And whan the fox saugh that he was y-gon,
'Allas!' quod he, 'O Chauntecleer, allas!
I have to yow,' quod he, 'y-doon trespas,   600

564 *Malkin*: a diminutive of Matilda and a conventional name for a serving maid.

569 *feendes*: the comparison is not without sinister implications. Representations of devils would have been familiar from church murals of the Last Judgement and – more importantly, given the stress on sound here – from the miracle plays, in which scenes from the Bible and Catholic theology were represented on Corpus Christi.

574 *Iakke Straw*: one of the leaders of the Peasants' Revolt of 1381 in which the people, invading London, sought freedom from outdated feudal laws and customs and from heavy taxation. London traders directed their forces against prosperous foreigners (the Flemings of l. 576). The revolt was both bloody and tragic.

583 *Lo, how fortune ...*: the theme of the instability of fortune (the Monk's theme) is reintroduced, but notice how the once proud Chauntecleer plays on the fox's vanity to escape. He frees himself from the jaws of death by a last-minute flash of shrewd intelligence. For a more detailed discussion, see Introduction, pp. 80–97.

593 *feith*: the use is ironic.

In-as-muche as I maked yow aferd,
Whan I yow hente, and broghte out of the yerd;
But, sire, I dide it in no wikke entente;
Com doun, and I shal telle yow what I mente.
I shal seye sooth to yow, god help me so.'
'Nay than,' quod he, 'I shrewe us bothe two.
And first I shrewe my-self, bothe blood and bones,
If thou bigyle me ofter than ones.
Thou shalt na-more, thurgh thy flaterye,
Do me to singe and winke with myn yĕ.   610
For he that winketh, whan he sholde see,
Al wilfully, god lat him never thee!'
'Nay,' quod the fox, 'but god yeve him meschaunce,
That is so undiscreet of governaunce,
That Iangleth whan he sholde holde his pees.'
    Lo, swich it is for to be recchelees,
And necligent, and truste on flaterye.
But ye that holden this tale a folye,
As of a fox, or of a cok and hen,
Taketh the moralitee, good men.   620
For seint Paul seith, that al that writen is,
To our doctryne it is y-write, y-wis.
Taketh the fruyt, and lat the chaf be stille.
    Now, gode god, if that it be thy wille,
As seith my lord, so make us alle good men;
And bringe us to his heighe blisse. Amen.

Here is ended the Nonne Preestes Tale.

609 *thurgh thy flaterye* . . .: Chauntecleer has freed himself from deception and is aware now of the metaphorical implications of closing his eyes.

615 *Iangleth*: the fox has learned his lesson too, but the intention is clearly ironic. What he says is also applicable to Chauntecleer.

616 *Lo, swich it is* . . .: this brief paragraph is enigmatic. The Nun's Priest's own description of his tale as a warning against carelessness, neglect of duty and trusting on flattery, while obviously applicable, is perhaps somewhat pat and simple, with the result that the 'moralitee' we are asked to take is none too obvious. His tale is far more than a simple homily. See Introduction, pp. 83–94.

The question of the tale as a 'folye' is also vexed. St Paul, writing to Timothy, gives three sharp warnings against giving heed to fables and old wives' tales and urging the exercise of godliness instead. However – and the wry irony is typical of the poem as a whole – the allusion made to St Paul in l. 621 is to Romans vx, 4, which declares that whatever things were written in the past were written for our instruction. It is, of course, the instruction the Nun's Priest asks us to take, thereby returning us to the problem of his 'moralitee'. It is interesting in this context that of the two priests who tell stories, the Nun's Priest tells a most dexterous and allusive fable, while the Parson, a figure to be wholly admired, is more rigid in his approach:

> This Persone him answerde, al at ones,
> 'Thou getest fable noon y-told for me;
> For Paul, that wryteth unto Timothee,
> Repreveth hem that weyven soothfastnesse,
> And tellen fables and swich wrecchednesse.

And, in fact, the Parson gives a sermon on the Seven Deadly Sins.

624 *Now, gode god* . . .: the prayer at the close is conventional and analogous to a sermon. The reference to 'my' lord remains ambiguous as Chaucer always refers to God (properly) as 'our' Lord.

Epilogue to the Nonne Preestes Tale

'Sir Nonnes Preest,' our hoste seyde anoon,
'Y-blessed be thy breche, and every stoon!
This was a mery tale of Chauntecleer.
But, by my trouthe, if thou were seculei,
Thou woldest been a trede-foul a-right.
For, if thou have corage as thou hast might,
Thee were nede of hennes, as I wene,
Ya, mo than seven tymes seventene.
See, whiche braunes hath this gentil Preest,
So greet a nekke, and swich a large breest!   10
He loketh as a sperhauk with his yën;
Him nedeth nat his colour for to dyen
With brasil, ne with greyn of Portingale.
Now sire, faire falle yow for youre tale!'
    And after that he, with ful mery chere,
Seide to another, as ye shullen here.

1   *'Sir Nonnes Preest ...*: The Epilogue, although not occurring in all manuscripts, is believed to be genuine. In it, the Nun's Priest is suddenly yet more alive for us as a full member of the pilgrimage party. However, it is noticeable that the Nun's Priest makes no reply to Harry Bailey's blunt comments and that the Host had also addressed similar remarks to the Monk. Indeed 1.5 here is repeated verbatim. Clerical celibacy was a debated issue, and in his address to the Monk, Harry Bailey regrets that virile men become ecclesiastics and so leave feebler men to engender children. He adds that it is because the clerics are so manly that married women run after them. Notice how, in Harry Bailey's remarks here, the Nun's Priest becomes – through his apparently libidinous nature – associated with birds. Evidently Harry Bailey sees traces of self-portraiture (or wish-fulfilment) in the Nun's Priest's picture of Chauntecleer.

2   *stoon*: testicles.

5   *trede-foul*: fornicating cockerel.

Reading List

Introductions to Chaucer, his life, times and *The Canterbury Tales* are legion. The following book list mainly contains works that help provide a context for *The Nun's Priest Tale* itself.

Bloomfield, Morton W., *The Seven Deadly Sins*, Michigan, 1952. The definitive work on this important subject.

Boethius, *The Consolation of Philosophy*, translated with an introduction by V. E. Watts, Harmondsworth, Penguin Books, 1969. Essential reading for all students of Chaucer.

Coleman, Janet, *1350–1400: Medieval Readers and Writers* ('English Literature in History' series, ed. Raymond Williams), London, Hutchinson, 1981. A useful guide to the political, social, religious and philosophical currents of the period and their relationship to literature.

Huizinga, J., *The Waning of the Middle Ages*, 1924, trans. F. Hopman, 1955, Harmondsworth, Penguin Books, 1955. An indispensible and great work of scholarship and imaginative insight.

Kolve, V. A., *Chaucer and the Imagery of Narrative*, London, Edward Arnold, 1984. Though not dealing with *The Nun's Priest's Tale* in detail, the work contains some interesting insights on Chaucer's symbolism.

Miller, J. M., Prosser, M. H., and Benson, T. W., eds., *Readings in Medieval Rhetoric*, Bloomington and London, Indiana University Press, 1973. A useful anthology.

Murphy, James J., *Rhetoric in the Middle Ages*, Berkeley, Los Angeles and London, University of California Press, 1974. An advanced study of an important area.

Myers, A. R., *England in the Late Middle Ages* ('The Pelican History of England' series), 8th edn, Harmondsworth, Penguin Books, 1971. A useful introduction to the social, political and intellectual backgrounds.

Pratt, Robert A., 'Some Latin Sources of the Nonnes Preest on Dreams', *Speculum*, 52 (1977), 538–70. Difficult to obtain, perhaps, but of great interest and importance.

Rowland, Beryl, *Blind Beasts: Chaucer's Animal World*, Ohio, Kent State University Press, 1971. A well-informed account of its interesting subject.

Sisam, Kenneth, ed., *The Nun's Priest's Tale*, Oxford, Clarendon Press, 1927. Useful, particularly on the sources.

Southern, R. W., *The Making of the Middle Ages*, Hutchinson, n.d. An indispensible work and a masterly introduction.

Glossary

a-right truly
abrayde woke up suddenly
abydeth remains
accordant in keeping with
Affrike Africa
agaste frighten
agayn opposite to, in
agu fever
als also
altercacioun division of opinion
amended improved
Andromacha Andromache (see textual note)
apoplexye a rush of blood to the head
apotecarie apothecary, chemist
areste arrest, restraint
arrayed got ready, prepared
arwes arrows
ascencioun rising above the horizon (see textual note)
assaille attack
asur blue
attamed began
attempree moderate
auctoritee authority, learning
auctours authors
Augustyn Augustine (see textual note)
avauntour boaster
aventure chance, luck
avisioun dream, vision
avoy alas
awayt wait

batailed crenellated
beer bore
bemes (l. 519) trumpets
bene bean, a worthless thing
benedicite Lord bless us
benefyce employment offered by the church
biggle trick
biknewe confessed
bile beak
bitokneth signifies
biwreyest reveal
blythe jolly
Boece Boethius (see textual note)
boles bulls
bon boxwood
boon bone
bord table
boteler butler
botme bottom, hull
bour bower, bedroom
Bradwardyn Bradwardine (see textual note)
brak broke
brasil red dye
brast broke
braunes muscles
breche breeches
bren bran
brend burned
brende burned
brent burned
briddes birds
brouke enjoy the use of
bulte sift
burned burnished

147

Burnel the Asse title of a poem (see textual note)

Cartage Carthage
cas mischance
casuelly by accident
catapace seed of catapuca tree (a purge)
catel capital, goods
Catoun Dionysius Cato (see textual note)
centaure centaury (a purge)
certes certainly
cherles common people
chuk cluck
Cipioun Scipio (see textual note)
clappeth chatters
clepe call
clerkes learned men
clos enclosure
col-fox fox with black markings
colde fatal, deathly
colera yellow bile (see textual note)
colerik choleric
commune in common
compaignable sociable
complecciouns temperaments (see textual note)
complet over
complexcioun blending of humours (see textual note)
contek strife
contrarie natural enemy
corage sexual vigour
corn grain of corn
cote cottage
counseil advice
countrefete imitate
cronique chronicle, history
curteys courteous (see textual note)

damoysele damsel, mistress
dan sir
daun master
daweninge dawning
debonaire gracious
deel bit, portion
del part
deliverly agilely
desport amusement
devyse describe
deye dairy keeper
discrecioun discernment
discreet prudent
disese discomfort
disputisoun argument
dissimilour dissembler
distaf distaff (cleft stick used for winding wool)
divyne perceive
doctryne teaching, betterment
dokes ducks
dong dung
dradde dreaded
drecched vexed, distressed
drede fear
dreynt drowned
dwelle linger
dyen dye
dyete diet

Ecclesiaste Ecclesiastes (in the Bible)
Ectores Hector (see textual note)
eek also
effect significance, consequences
ellebor hellebore (a purge)
elles else
endyte compose, set down
Eneydos Aeneid (Virgil)
engendren derive
engyned tortured on the rack

entente intention

eny any

equinoxial time when the sun crosses the equator (see textual note)

erbe yve buck's horn (a cure for fever)

eschewed avoided

estaat state, condition, rank

everichon everyone, each and all

expouned taught the meaning of

ey egg

eyled ailed, made wrong

fader father

faren in londe gone away

fayn delighted

felawe companion

felonye crime

fere fear

fethered copulated (of birds)

flatour flatterer

fleigh flew

fley flew

folye foolish thing

fond provided for

for-sleuthen lose through delay

forn-cast forecast, predicted

fors, do no take no notice of

forwiting foreknowledge

forwoot foreknows

free open

fro from

fume vapour rising from stomach

fumetere fumitory (a purge)

gabbe tell a lie

galwes gallows

game fun, as a joke

gape gasp in agony

gargat throat

Gaufred Geoffrey of Vinsauf (see textual note)

gaytres buckthorn berries (a purge)

Genilon Ganelon (see textual note)

gentil well-bred

gilt sin

gladsom cheering

governaunce control; self-control (l. 614)

greyn of Portingale scarlet dye from Portugal

grote, leye a wager a groat (fourpence)

habounde was learned

habundant abundant

halle living room

han have

hap chance

hardy tough; brave

harrow a cry for help

Hasdrubales Hasdrubal (see textual note)

haven-syde shore of an inlet or harbour

heed concern

hegges hedges

hele healing, health

heled concealed

hente seized

herbergage accommodation

hertelees coward

hertely earnestly

hevinesse sorrow, grief

hewed coloured

highte called

ho halt

iade a horse of poor quality

Iakke Straw a leader of the Peasants' Revolt

iangleth chatters
iapes jokes, tricks
ieet jet
Ilioun Troy
imaginacioun imagination, insight
iniquiteee malice
in principio in the beginning

kepe protect, watch over
kinde natural properties or skills
kyn cows

leste pleased
lette stay; delay (l. 214)
lever rather
lief love
liggen lie
lith (l. 55) limb, part
logge lodging
loken locked, bound
lorn lost, killed
losengeour deceiver
lust desire
Lyde Lydia (see textual note)
lyte little

maad made
Macrobeus Macrobius (see textual note)
maistow may you
malencolye melancholy, black bile (see textual note)
mase delusion (but see textual note)
maugree despite
Mercenrike Saxon kingdom of Mercia
mervaille marvel
mery delightful
meschaunce unhappiness
meschief trouble

messe-days days for laymen's masses
met dreamed
mette dreamt, dreamed
meynee crowd of followers
ministres magistrates; officers of justice
mochel much
moder mother
moralitee moral, meaning
mordre murder
morwe-tyde morning
mot must

na-more no more
narwe small, mean
nas there was not
nature natural instinct
necessitee condicionel events in which man has some degree of choice
necligent negligent
nedely necessarily
nere were it not for
nigard miser
nones, for the there and then
noon no, none
noot know not
notabilitee noteworthy fact
nourice nurse
ny nearly
nyce foolish

o a single
orlogge clock
out-sterte ran out
outrely completely

paramours mistresses
parde by the Lord
pasture meal, feeding

150

peer equal
perfit complete, highly educated
pestilence plague
peyne exert
Phisiologus title of a book (see Introduction)
phisyk medicine
Pirrus Pyrrhus (see textual note)
plat plainly
plesaunce pleasure
plese give pleasure
Poules St Paul's Cathedral
pouped blew
povre poor
poynaunt sharply flavoured
poynt detail
preve practical test
prively secretly
prow benefit
pryme six in the morning; period between 6 and 9 a.m.
pyned tortured

quelle kill
quod said

recche read, interpret
recchelees careless, unheeding
recckelees careless
regnes kings
rekke care
remes realms
rennen ran
rente income
repaire go to frequently
repleccioun over-eating
replecciouns (l. 103) excesses
repleet overfull
rethor rhetorician (see Introduction)
revel happiness, desire for pleasure

reweth makes me sorry
right quite
roghte heeded
rude blunt
ryde mount

saufly safely
say saw
Scariot Judas Iscariot (see textual note)
science knowledge
sclendre modest
scole university philosophy school
secree discreet
seculer a man not in religious orders
seints holy
sely innocent, humble, good
sentence opinion, instruction; meaning (l. 345)
sewed saw
seynd smoked
shadde poured
shaltow you shall
shente injured
shrewe curse
shrighte shrieked
shryked shrieked
significaciouns signs, warnings
siker sure, trustworthy
sikerly truly
simple necessitee inevitable events, such as death
sin since
slawe slew
slough hollow, ditch
slow slew
smal narrow
snowte muzzle
sodeyn sudden
solas pleasure

somdel somewhat
sond sand
sooth true
soothfastnesse truth
sorwe sorrow
sovereyn supreme
sperhauk sparrow hawk
stalle shed
stape advanced
stente wait, delay
stevene voice
stinte stop, leave aside
stoon testicles
streit (l. 169) limited, restricted
streyneth constrains, obliges
substance natural ability to
   respond favourably
suffisaunce contentment
suffre allow
superfluitee excess
sustres sisters
swete charming
swevene dream
swevenis dreams
swich such

terciane a fever manifesting itself
   on alternate days
tespye spy out
thilke that
tho those
thritty thirty
tool weapon
toon toes

unwar unforeseen

vanitee emptiness, nothing at all
venimous poisonous, distasteful
verray real, sound
viage journey
vileinye harm, dishonesty

wende knew
wesh wash
wexeth grows
weylaway alas
whelpes dogs
wher-as where that, when
whylom once
widwe widow
wight person
wikke evil
winke close the eyes
with-oute on the outside
witing knowing
wlatsom ugly, revolting
wolde would
woldestow would you, did you
wonder wonderfully
woned lived
wont in the habit of
woot knows
wortes vegetables
wroght done

y-logged lodged
y-wis certainly
y-write written
yen eyes
yit yet
yon play

FOR THE BEST IN PAPERBACKS, LOOK FOR THE

In every corner of the world, on every subject under the sun, Penguin represents quality and variety – the very best in publishing today.

For complete information about books available from Penguin – including Pelicans, Puffins, Peregrines and Penguin Classics – and how to order them, write to us at the appropriate address below. Please note that for copyright reasons the selection of books varies from country to country.

In the United Kingdom: For a complete list of books available from Penguin in the U.K., please write to *Dept E.P., Penguin Books Ltd, Harmondsworth, Middlesex, UB7 0DA*

In the United States: For a complete list of books available from Penguin in the U.S., please write to *Dept BA, Penguin, 299 Murray Hill Parkway, East Rutherford, New Jersey 07073*

In Canada: For a complete list of books available from Penguin in Canada, please write to *Penguin Books Canada Ltd, 2801 John Street, Markham, Ontario L3R 1B4*

In Australia: For a complete list of books available from Penguin in Australia, please write to the *Marketing Department, Penguin Books Australia Ltd, P.O. Box 257, Ringwood, Victoria 3134*

In New Zealand: For a complete list of books available from Penguin in New Zealand, please write to the *Marketing Department, Penguin Books (NZ) Ltd, Private Bag, Takapuna, Auckland 9*

In India: For a complete list of books available from Penguin, please write to *Penguin Overseas Ltd, 706 Eros Apartments, 56 Nehru Place, New Delhi, 110019*

In Holland: For a complete list of books available from Penguin in Holland, please write to *Penguin Books Nederland B.V., Postbus 195, NL–1380AD Weesp, Netherlands*

In Germany: For a complete list of books available from Penguin, please write to *Penguin Books Ltd, Friedrichstrasse 10 – 12, D–6000 Frankfurt Main 1, Federal Republic of Germany*

In Spain: For a complete list of books available from Penguin in Spain, please write to *Longman Penguin España, Calle San Nicolas 15, E–28013 Madrid, Spain*

FOR THE BEST IN PAPERBACKS, LOOK FOR THE

PENGUIN CLASSICS

Saint Anselm	The Prayers and Meditations
Saint Augustine	The Confessions
Bede	A History of the English Church and People
Chaucer	The Canterbury Tales
	Love Visions
	Troilus and Criseyde
Froissart	The Chronicles
Geoffrey of Monmouth	The History of the Kings of Britain
Gerald of Wales	History and Topography of Ireland
	The Journey through Wales and The Description of Wales
Gregory of Tours	The History of the Franks
Julian of Norwich	Revelations of Divine Love
William Langland	Piers the Ploughman
Sir John Mandeville	The Travels of Sir John Mandeville
Marguerite de Navarre	The Heptameron
Christine de Pisan	The Treasure of the City of Ladies
Marco Polo	The Travels
Richard Rolle	The Fire of Love
Thomas à Kempis	The Imitation of Christ

ANTHOLOGIES AND ANONYMOUS WORKS

The Age of Bede
Alfred the Great
Beowulf
A Celtic Miscellany
The Cloud of Unknowing and Other Works
The Death of King Arthur
The Earliest English Poems
Early Christian Writings
Early Irish Myths and Sagas
Egil's Saga
The Letters of Abelard and Heloise
Medieval English Verse
Njal's Saga
Seven Viking Romances
Sir Gawain and the Green Knight
The Song of Roland

PENGUIN CLASSICS

Pedro de Alarcón	**The Three-Cornered Hat and Other Stories**
Leopoldo Alas	**La Regenta**
Ludovico Ariosto	**Orlando Furioso**
Giovanni Boccaccio	**The Decameron**
Baldassar Castiglione	**The Book of the Courtier**
Benvenuto Cellini	**Autobiography**
Miguel de Cervantes	**Don Quixote**
	Exemplary Stories
Dante	**The Divine Comedy** (in 3 volumes)
	La Vita Nuova
Bernal Diaz	**The Conquest of New Spain**
Carlo Goldoni	**Four Comedies (The Venetian Twins/The Artful Widow/Mirandolina/The Superior Residence)**
Niccolo Machiavelli	**The Discourses**
	The Prince
Alessandro Manzoni	**The Betrothed**
Giorgio Vasari	**Lives of the Artists** (in 2 volumes)

and

Five Italian Renaissance Comedies (Machiavelli/The Mandragola; Ariosto/Lena; Aretino/The Stablemaster; Gl'Intronatie/The Deceived;Guarini/The Faithful Shepherd)
The Jewish Poets of Spain
The Poem of the Cid
Two Spanish Picaresque Novels (Anon/Lazarillo de Tormes; de Quevedo/The Swindler)

FOR THE BEST IN PAPERBACKS, LOOK FOR THE

PENGUIN CLASSICS

Klaus von Clausewitz	**On War**
Friedrich Engels	**The Origins of the Family, Private Property and the State**
Wolfram von Eschenbach	**Parzival**
	Willehalm
Goethe	**Elective Affinities**
	Faust
	Italian Journey 1786–88
Jacob and Wilhelm Grimm	**Selected Tales**
E. T. A. Hoffmann	**Tales of Hoffmann**
Henrik Ibsen	**The Doll's House/The League of Youth/The Lady from the Sea**
	Ghosts/A Public Enemy/When We Dead Wake
	Hedda Gabler/The Pillars of the Community/The Wild Duck
	The Master Builder/Rosmersholm/Little Eyolf/John Gabriel Borkman/ Peer Gynt
Søren Kierkegaard	**Fear and Trembling**
Friedrich Nietzsche	**Beyond Good and Evil**
	Ecce Homo
	A Nietzsche Reader
	Thus Spoke Zarathustra
	Twilight of the Idols and **The Anti-Christ**
Friedrich Schiller	**The Robbers** and **Wallenstein**
Arthur Schopenhauer	**Essays and Aphorisms**
Gottfried von Strassburg	**Tristan**
August Strindberg	**Inferno** and **From an Occult Diary**

Anton Chekhov	The Duel and Other Stories
	The Kiss and Other Stories
	Lady with Lapdog and Other Stories
	Plays (The Cherry Orchard/Ivanov/The Seagull/Uncle Vanya/The Bear/The Proposal/A Jubilee/Three Sisters
	The Party and Other Stories
Fyodor Dostoyevsky	The Brothers Karamazov
	Crime and Punishment
	The Devils
	The Gambler/Bobok/A Nasty Story
	The House of the Dead
	The Idiot
	Netochka Nezvanova
	Notes From Underground and The Double
Nikolai Gogol	Dead Souls
	Diary of a Madman and Other Stories
Maxim Gorky	My Apprenticeship
	My Childhood
	My Universities
Mikhail Lermontov	A Hero of Our Time
Alexander Pushkin	Eugene Onegin
	The Queen of Spades and Other Stories
Leo Tolstoy	Anna Karenin
	Childhood/Boyhood/Youth
	The Cossacks/The Death of Ivan Ilyich/Happy Ever After
	The Kreutzer Sonata and Other Stories
	Master and Man and Other Stories
	Resurrection
	The Sebastopol Sketches
	War and Peace
Ivan Turgenev	Fathers and Sons
	First Love
	Home of the Gentry

FOR THE BEST IN PAPERBACKS, LOOK FOR THE 🐧

PENGUIN CLASSICS

Basho	**The Narrow Road to the Deep North**
	On Love and Barley
Cao Xuequin	**The Story of the Stone** *also known as* **The Dream**
	of the Red Chamber (in five volumes)
Confucius	**The Analects**
Khayyam	**The Ruba'iyat of Omar Khayyam**
Lao Tzu	**Tao Te Ching**
Li Po/Tu Fu	**Li Po and Tu Fu**
Sei Shōnagon	**The Pillow Book of Sei Shōnagon**
Wang Wei	**Poems**

Anthologies and Anonymous Works
The Bhagavad Gita
Buddhist Scriptures
The Dhammapada
Hindu Myths
The Koran
New Songs from a Jade Terrace
The Rig Veda
Speaking of Śiva
Tales from the Thousand and One Nights
The Upanishads